ANGULAR DESIRE

Srinivas Rayaprol was born in 1925 in Secunderabad. He studied at Nizam College, Hyderabad, and Banaras Hindu University before going to Stanford University from where he obtained a masters in Civil Engineering. While in the US, he started writing poetry in English and interacted closely with writers like William Carlos Williams, Yvor Winters and James Laughlin. His correspondence with Williams has been published as *Why Should I Write a Poem Now: The Letters of Srinivas Rayaprol and William Carlos Williams, 1949–1958* (2018), edited by Graziano Krätli. His books of poetry include *Bones and Distances* (1968), *Married Love and Other Poems* (1972) and *Selected Poems* (1995).

Graziano Krätli is a translator, editor and author based in Connecticut, USA, where he works as a librarian at Yale University. He has published articles and reviews on literary subjects, particularly modern and contemporary anglophone literature in India, as well as articles on manuscript production, circulation and preservation in West Africa. He is the co-editor of *The Trans-Saharan Book Trade: Manuscript Culture, Arabic Literacy and Intellectual History in Muslim Africa* (2010) and the editor of *Why Should I Write a Poem Now: The Letters of Srinivas Rayaprol and William Carlos Williams, 1949-1958* (2018) and *Random Harvest*, the Indian edition of Rayaprol's selected poems and prose (forthcoming).

Vidyan Ravinthiran is an Associate Professor at Harvard University, and the author of two books of poetry, as well as *Elizabeth Bishop's Prosaic* (Bucknell UP, 2015), winner of both the University English Prize and the Warren-Brooks Award for Outstanding Literary Criticism.

SRINIVAS RAYAPROL

Angular Desire

SELECTED POEMS AND PROSE

edited by
GRAZIANO KRÄTLI &
VIDYAN RAVINTHIRAN

CARCANET

First published in Great Britain in 2020 by
Carcanet
Alliance House, 30 Cross Street
Manchester M2 7AQ
www.carcanet.co.uk

A CIP catalogue record for this book is
available from the British Library.
ISBN 978 1 78410 925 7

Printed in Great Britain by SRP Ltd, Exeter, Devon

The publisher acknowledges financial
assistance from Arts Council England.

CONTENTS

TRANSLATIONS

PROSE

PREFACE

There are any number of reasons why we keep reading a writer – where I say 'read', one might add 'publish', 'review' and 'teach' – and yet the truest goal must be an experience of literary complexity. A style of thinking contingent upon their uniquely disposed forms. Postcolonial literature is insufficiently considered as art. In fact, there are those for whom aesthetics seem fatuous, beside the point, or, worse, one of the disguises worn by hegemonic power. But I don't agree. And, in fact, I think it's about time that authors from underrepresented, and misrepresented, communities were taken seriously as *writers* – not witnesses unto atrocity, or speaking wounds.

Srinivas Rayaprol's verse, and prose, has to it a peculiarly hightailing swiftness that – resembling Louis MacNeice, whom he met – makes discoveries as it goes:

> For me it was the step yesterday
> That makes me see
> That the release I've always sought
> The knot I've wished to unknot
> Is nothing more
> Than the crab's dignity in the sand
> ('Crabs in the Seine')

'For me' qualifies what is to follow: we bounce from the past into the present, and back again; 'the awful daring' of, in T.S. Eliot's phrase, 'a moment's surrender' coexists with fatalistic processes. Rayaprol devises with his syntax and lineation a 'knot' – one of, as Graziano Krätli writes in the afterword, his key images – which, unlike the Gordian one, can't simply be cut asunder. You can't paraphrase, that is, these cussedly tortuous lines, which are also a movement of thought, or the opposite – a stalling action which remains totally compelling.

The problem is this. Rayaprol writes strong poems and weak ones, and, worse, even the intertextures of his best poems can fray. Graziano and I worked with, to produce this edition, texts mobbed by misprints and skew-whiff English, not all of which can be blamed on his editors. The poems evince, when they become unidiomatic or phrasally clenched, an Indian English distinctively his. He writes of an emotional disorder which his language to some extent reproduces, but with felicities that imply deliberation. This seems to me the big question: are the poems consciously (not haplessly) wonky? I think so, though I also prize in them a voice that isn't wholly and perpetually self-secure, that expresses without undue defensiveness a hybrid intelligence informed, and deformed, by both Indian living and US writing.

During and after his stint in the States, Rayaprol was nourished by his friendship with William Carlos Williams ('when in the winter of 1950 I found myself in New York on a winter vacation, I wrote to Dr Williams that I would like to meet him… though he had mis-spelt my name, his welcome was warm and genuine'). He learned from that poet to forgo crypsis, to detail sincerely, and to be explorative rather than confirmatory in his lineation:

Each night the flesh moves
its heavy weight on the air
and at morning the distant

wall of a broken barn breaks
through the nightlong snow.

From night, to morning, and then back to 'nightlong' – the mixed time-signatures do so much, but I was stuck to explain the force upon me of 'Here It Is Spring Again' until I read 'Yesterday': a poem about US race-relations, spoken from the perspective of an African-American woman and bus-passengers 'with blank eyes / and unlovely faces', who won't sit next to her (only a blind man does). 'Unlovely' took me back to Tennyson, and a lyric from *In Memoriam:*

> Dark house, by which once more I stand
> Here in the long unlovely street [...]
>
> He is not here; but far away
> The noise of life begins again,
> And ghastly thro' the drizzling rain
> On the bald street breaks the blank day.[1]

Rayaprol engages unconventionally with the developments of Anglo-American modernism, but his reading goes back still further: words and sounds ('bald street breaks'; 'broken barn breaks') migrate – I can think of no better word, for doctors also use it to describe the transference of pain from one limb to another – out of Tennyson's verse and into his. When the image recurs in 'Pastorale' – 'the first broken wall of a barn / broke the rhythm that monotony / sometimes has on the moving eye' – we see that his enquiry into perception is also, as in Williams, a self-consciousness of poetic style.

These borrowings need to be distinguished from the sentimental copy-and-pasting by Indian poets writing in English, of the banalities of Victorian and Edwardian verse. Rajeev Patke tells us that nineteenth-century poetry was

1 *The Oxford Authors: Alfred Tennyson*, ed. Adam Roberts (Oxford: OUP, 2000), 208.

'diligently imitative'; what you get from the colonised's first attempts at artistic originality is 'mimicry, incongruity, and ineptness'.[2] In his memoir, *The True Paradise*, the Sri Lankan writer and critic Gamini Salgado tells of being defended, absurdly, in court, for playing truant. At first glance, his lawyer appears to speak the kind of malformed, wordy, and in Arvind Mehrotra's phrase, 'babu' English which has evolved grotesquely out of what the Raj left behind. But we realise that this scatter-plot of fevered citations from Palgrave's *Treasury* is in fact quite brilliantly constructed, as de Silva (hired with a couple of rupees the boy was meant to spend on biryani at a cricket match) preens in court as marvellously as Oscar Wilde:

> 'Your Honour, we have here a truly piteous case of oppression and harassment. Consider this young lad setting off at break of day with shining morning face, eager to arrive at his alma mater and there imbibe the invigorating waters of learning from the Pyrennean springs.'
>
> The magistrate looked imploringly at Mr de Silva but he was too far gone for imploring looks.
>
> 'Education, Your Honour, is the inalienable right of every citizen of this resplendent isle. It is the cornerstone of our democratic system, the stepping stone on which each and every one of us rises from our dead self to fresh fields and pastures new.'[3]

It's funny but there's a point to it, because English was, and perhaps remains, an aspirational matter to Indians and Sri Lankans, a 'stepping stone' to power: magnificently authoritative, it seems to promise, if conquered and internalised, an eloquence that would put one forever beyond

2 *Postcolonial Poetry in English* (Oxford: OUP, 2009), 59.

3 *The True Paradise*, ed. Fenella Copplestone (Manchester: Carcanet, 1993), 94.

harm. The slave dreams of taking the master's language, and, with it, his magic.

Rayaprol is never so boring as to put the point so plainly (I doubt, in fact, that he could put anything plainly) but it's worth considering 'white', as it appears in his poems. It is often applied, as above, to snow, with which he's obsessed – having never seen it, one imagines, before coming to the US – but which he often turns into an abstract 'white' weight descending from the sky. Yet he also writes frankly, sexually, of complexions:

> Fat old men with flat white faces
> That shine out of the pages of *Time*
>   And speak to me
>
> Of the unspeakable pleasures possible
> Between our bodies.
> ('All Kinds of Love')
>
> [...]
>
> I speak not of the mystery that is woman
> Nor of the great white being that is God –
> I do not speak of love, or of people,
> For I have known neither father nor lover
> And none have I reached with what I cannot utter.
>
> But I speak of the lonely word
> That will not reach beyond my tongue
> Nor fulfill my frustrations.
> ('This Poem')

Sexuality can also be a matter of aspiration, to reach a locus of power and fame – this is what *Time* magazine stands for – where all one's yearnings will convert, like caterpillars becoming butterflies, into a banquet of unanxious pleasures. 'Many years ago, when I was about seventeen or eighteen, my one ambition was to be a great poet, but I did not know what it meant except to thrill at a line of Auden or a word of Wallace Stevens, and imagine the unimaginable – that one day I, too, would join the galaxy. Poets were lonely people, I had heard, and was I not the loneliest of the lonely?' As an Indian immigrant (and then an Indian back home) it was harder for Rayaprol than for others to 'speak' of his homosexual feelings, but the slap-bang candour of the first poem, and the contrary hauteur (the inversions, the syntax) of the second suggest that it was never easy for him to 'speak', in his verse at least, on any subject. There were always obstacles, and he couldn't make up his mind whether to glide above them in the passenger-jet of a refined high style, or to make his way on foot (again, like Williams), incorporating into his poetics the textures of the terrain.

Can a frustration be 'fulfilled'? Perhaps: it's another of those moments where we see Rayaprol seeking the foothold of a received phrase, or the contour of a pre-existing idiom, only to veer towards a perhaps unintended originality. He admired in the painter Jamini Roy that 'at a certain stage of his life, he had the courage to discard everything he knew and had learned as an artist, and to plunge in the dark: a certain light within his head must have been his only direction.' Rayaprol's prose suggests of his own plunging verse that we're concerned here with a wholesale experimentalism, a risking of the basic unit of coherence. A refusal to turn the project of self-understanding into self-assuagement:

> I have never been more
> than the occasion demanded

have never been in an occasion
which demanded more than me

I have never had the mind's argument
dislodged by the horses of the heart

have never ridden horses
which did not know their riders
('Poem for a Birthday')

Because the English words are strange to him, Rayaprol inhabits his first idea like Hamlet having nightmares within a nutshell. He tries out a phrase, turns it inside out, seeking a mathematical equivalency; projecting an ideal fit between a person and his environment (an immigrant's dream) he begins to realise that what is lost from such a zero-sum game is personality itself. We might think 'riders' is another typo (should it be 'rider'?) but the point may be that you can never ride the same horse, just as you can never step in the same river, more than once: there are an infinite number of both horses and riders.

Returning to India, and becoming a civil engineer, Rayaprol wasn't happy. It could be he needed to be on the move, to (like Larkin in Ireland) at some level not belong. Certainly, his one masterpiece, 'Poem' (his titles are revealing, the hurriedly-applied labels of try-outs in test-tubes, haphazardly shelved) seems to me a love-letter to those who, rooted in the one place, grow identical with it; but also a sort of prayer – you can hear it as you read, a countermelody – to never be that person:

In India
Women

Have a way
Of growing old

My mother
For instance

Sat on the floor
A hundred years

Stirring soup
In a sauce-pan

Sometimes staring
At the bitter neem tree in the yard

For a hundred years
Within the kitchen walls.

Not a word is out of place: the woman, 'my mother', is exactly where, it would seem, she belongs; how does she feel about it? The transferred epithet 'bitter', the trick done, once again, with time – so Rayaprol seems to present us all at once with a visionary instant, and also a grief-stricken duration – it's a poem to anthologise, and canonise, and there are many others here which deserve to be read the world over.

Vidyan Ravinthiran

NOTE ON THE TEXT

Despite his decade-long epistolary relationship with William Carlos Williams, who provided long-distance mentoring and occasionally commented upon his literary efforts, Rayaprol's poetry suffered from the lack of critical readers and serious editing, let alone adequate copy-editing and proof-reading. This accounts for most peculiarities of diction and typographical errors (the latter more often than not introduced by Indian typesetters without a proper – or, indeed, any – knowledge of English) that we find in his three collections of verse, *Bones and Distances* (1968), *Married Love and Other Poems* (1972) and *Selected Poems* (1995), all published by Writers Workshop of Calcutta (now Kolkata). In the absence of original manuscripts, except for the handful of typescripts Rayaprol enclosed with his letters, these three books and the magazines in which some of the poems were first printed provide all the available copy. This is what we used to compare versions, clarify discrepancies and make any necessary corrections.

Most inconsistencies occur between the first two collections and the third, which shows instances of authorial revision but also introduces new errors. While the errors were a non-issue, we frequently pondered the revisions, and in a number of cases ended up choosing the original over the 'revised' version.

A more extensive form of revision concerned capitalisation, which is inconsistent in all three collections, but especially in *Selected Poems*. In this case our approach was, essentially, to assess the 'inclination' of the poem, and to act accordingly. So, if the pattern was to capitalise with the punctuation, we applied this method consistently throughout the poem; otherwise we capitalised the first letter of every line or no letter at all (except in the case of proper names), depending on what we understood to be the original intentions of the author.

Rayaprol's poetry appears to be affected by a light version of what Mark Twain called, with respect to the German language, a 'compounding-disease'. His inclination to coin compound adjectives, both in the closed and hyphenated forms, produced specimens like 'harshwood', 'flowerblind', 'rainwalked streets', 'man-walked streams', 'cheery-eyed', 'fish-white eye', 'river-ache', and 'leaf-left frailty', among others. A relatively short poem like 'The Peter Grimes of Benjamin Britten' features 'riverache', 'surfbreaks', 'wailmouth', 'rockhungry' (plus the neologism 'raucologues'). The most felicitous results of this tendency may be attributed to the young poet's experimentation with modernist prosody and the American idiom, while an English-language purist would probably write off the others as Hinglish freaks.

This latter interpretation notwithstanding, we kept most closed compounds except for those that were hyphenated in *Selected Poems*.

Rayaprol's close-compounding inclination muddles the meaning of the first stanza of 'Under the Bo-Tree', which in all known versions reads 'White loads fell from the sky on his winter body / Yellow leaves spread sunfull desires on his skin.' In the original typescript, enclosed to a letter to Williams dated 10 June 1950, Rayaprol wrote 'sunfill', a typo obviously although one that leaves both alternatives – 'sunfilled' or 'sinful' – open. The situation is further complicated by the fact that, a later poem, 'Some Thoughts on Trees', ends with virtually the same lines ('white loads have fallen from the sky / and my wishes are winter men // yellow leaves have spread'), except that it cuts out the last line and the reader is left wondering what the 'yellow leaves have spread' or where. Was this omission a mistake? Was the whole repetition? Of course, 'sunfull' (or sun-filled) desires may be sinful for an ascetic who is about to attain enlightenment; and the orthographic affinities and possible semantic relationship between 'sun-filled', 'sunfull' and 'sinful' is conducive to various considerations on the need, the purposes and the limits of hyphenation. But this is beyond the scope of this note.

Finally, we restored the names of less known dedicatees who originally featured in *Bones and Distances* but were dropped from *Selected Poems*.

POEMS

THE RAIN

fell like lice
on the running dogs
and cracked like pox
on the pavement men

It walked some walls
and ran thru gutters
gathered in lazy pools
in the hollow places

and hurried down
the asphalt ways

moistened the rags
of my soul and
knocked softly
on my windowpane.

UNTITLED *(fragment)*

Why should I write a poem Now
that most of me is dead
in the act of living

That the long fingered trees which reached
the snow to my early bed
stand now rooted to the earth...

UNTITLED

Is this then the reality
You'd have me know?
That the one I last saw
Hair blown in the wind, eyes
Mixed with a happiness
That was also sadness
Will not be there to smile again?
Only, spare me the details
There was a dog I saw, once,
Beneath the wheels, in the past
And the smallest reference
Brings back the picture
A broken leg hovering for air
The blood and the hair
And the curiosity of the crowds

DOGS IN RUIN

Go love!
rainclouds hang sad in the sky
and dogs need direction in life

The flower has missed the bee
and the garden ruined the gardener

When you die could you see
what I would of you

You must live as you would wish
to face your death

You must love the object
as you would the idea

Go love,
where the bougainvillea blooms
its inconstant yellow
against the colourless sky
The rain falls cold, love
on your face,
for the moon has missed his moods
and you have succeeded in achieving failure

Go love, do not let
go love for love is all
for a dog in the rain

FOUR LOVE POEMS

1.
Love is all
But only
In the particular moment

Of surrender or deceit
Or the close coition
Of a desire
That is not desire

Love is all
But only
For the eye
That sees

Or the dormant hand
In the heart
That stirs
The privacy of pain.

2.
And a lost road
Has brought me this way
The blind girl smiled
As she held my deceptive hand

A thousand sheep bled
Beneath my harshwood stave
While her flowerblind hand
Held my cloth of rucksack and skin

You are He, her lips smiled
Her idiot eye on my body
I, casual, indifferent
Took her on the mountain slopes

And left her the mud brown day

3.
Child, she said,
Be outside my love
For I bear the burden
Of your iniquities
Just like your father
In anger and in love
Find in me only
The receptacle for your deceits

While constant I stand
Helpless in love
And my unwilling womb
Accepts your cruelties.

4.
Remember when as children
We slept in our grandmother's coffin
A box of oak with camphor smells
And the rose in your hair crushed within

Grown now and forgotten
In memory's green sorrow
And the mildewed breath of insincerity
We sleep in our own

And I can see beside me
Your uncomfortable face, and our jaded bliss
Showing like cancer spots
Beneath the rose leaf

Smoke brown flames
Across the flat white moon
And time passes like a knotted hand
Before the window bar's golden bloom

The eye that lies beneath the object's delight
The heart that beats behind the clocking heart
Is but a small sufficiency
For the ingrown sin in the bone.

CRABS IN THE SEINE

for Mary Mereness

Flow softly sweet Seine
Maldoror is melancholy again
Between chimney teeth the eaten moon glows
Between the bird's freedom and the bird's flight
Maldoror sits counting the lines of rain.

I thought I knew you
For forty years
There was no question of not knowing
Of not being known
And yet only yesterday
Coming down the stairs
In some hurry
I missed a step

Did not fall your face rose
To my eyes and I asked,
What is she?

Really no question at all
It was like opening a door
Knowing that beyond were other doors
And the emptiness far
As the step I missed yesterday
For there was love
And in the dark I have felt your familiar weight
Each separate part a known delicacy
So finite at times vulgar

And in the lighted hall how often
Have I been blind to your dullness
One can be sure of love, it is an infliction
We impose on ourselves to release certain
Vague desires. A selfish volcano
That ignores the destruction beyond
Its satisfied interior

And I thought I knew you
All these years, your few favourites
Your private peeves, the turn
Of your body in fear, the swivel
Of your neck in love
Forty years is a long habit

But one arrives somehow
Often beyond one's willing
At certain lonely graves
That ask the unaskable

What do I know of you
What do I know of myself that I can say?
We are made for each other and indulge
In the common talk that people in love
Invoke to satisfy their lacks

For me it was the step yesterday
That makes me see
That the release I've always sought
The knot I've wished to unknot
Is nothing more
Than the crab's dignity in the sand

The flying bird flies
In a controlled orbit
Circumference without centre
Is not the freedom what
Is sought by the flying bird
As it flies into the air
Between the bird's motion
And the base that fixes it
Is an understanding

And the nets we weave around ourselves
The rope you used yesterday
Is the only hope
I ever had for the time being
The rope having slipped
The release in my groin, in my head, in my body
Is for me now quite void

What hurts my dear is not your death
But that going you removed the centre
And left me free and tearless.

ORANGES ON A TABLE

for Kenneth Pettitt

acquire
the subtle distinction
of mahogany.

No longer
a thought
on the tree
in spring

but nude
as green
its body
a summer-arm

yellow and slow
woman-close.

Not an ultimate order
of the orange sky

but the angular
desire

of the stone
that blocks
the river's run

LETTER TO EZRA POUND

for William Carlos Williams

Not the shadow filled tomorrow
nor the last night's hesitant recede
but the present.
Always the immigrant now
in the heart
where dissatisfaction builds
like sea kelp.

Break a branch without
the window and flower
it within this room
in the precise bottle of prussic acid

And if the rose does bloom
Is it but an old man's old mind?

Ah, dear Ezra, how thine head
burns in the grate, beside
the flower that beds slowly –
and Bill, moist-eyed, old-shaken
sings of your cruel jests
your swollen head and your utter
lack of consideration.

Sing William sing
for a lost playmate
now cheery-eyed, now stubborn, now
unbelieving behind bars
conjuring Chinese rhymes and ancient myth

Sing William sing
a sudden tear
for the only fish in the only pond,
lonely, lonely Ezra Pound.

ON GROWING OLD

There is a manner of growing old
A manner much like trees
That pass from day to night
Clocking the seasons, breeding
New desires for the inquiring eye
Themselves transitionless
In grief or green
And still.

And a manner not like women
Gold in their mouth, glaze
In their eyes, the similar glitter
Of an illusion of the past
That was not the real past
But a remembered one,
Or a remembered one
Self-deceiving and concupiscent
As the moon
On flat white faces
Behind plate-glass windows

Not shedding like a tree
In age its gaudy acquisitions
Not shooting the sap
But containing it

An even yellow
Manner of growing old
Like trees
Like women.

A LETTER FOR MOTHER

For heaven's sake, mother,
how you've aged!
You could have been kinder.

Roots twist
and the rinse
of leaves under rain
has different smells;
white loads them
differently
and the sun sets
a new yellow.
Trees grow old too.

Couldn't you crust your kindness
in another way?

Wormwood and water decay
in your mouth
your body is a dried river
and your eye
a seamy stream
of undone sins.

But not in the same way,
you'll say,
the modus of trees
is different.
The white snow is white
and the seeing eye black
you're still my golden boy
and I
your beautiful bride
neither the barked tree
nor the burning axe
are at fault
for the center
is not here.

Mother, do not kiss me,
for Heaven's sake,
your lips are leavenings
and mine withered ants.

You could have been kinder
separate yourself from your oldness.
The return is not the end
and hope only in the waiting.

LES SALTIMBANQUES

Simply say
The mute clown yonder
And the sufficient singer there
Are the living ghosts, at the eye's
Concupiscent remove

The private part played
For the public eye
Which is always the self.

The laugh we stopped
And the tear that never broke
Its eye, the impotent
Excitement
Of our normal lives
Lies in seeking
Them elsewhere.

BONES AND DISTANCES

And so each day
with a shaking of hands
begins a part
a new part for every
corresponding gesture
of the body.

Some new lie to be conjured
some unhappened glory to enrich
our normality, a new fitting word
for the just-worn suit.

And so there is the moment
for every man, the moment
out of space, between the clocks

the moment within and without
the self, when perhaps
happily in sleep

to escape from life…

But what then of the thousand
letters unanswered, the sunshine
and the trees,
what of the million conversations
with your million parts

when to escape
from desire
and the million doubts
of being born.

POEM FOR A BIRTHDAY

I have never been more
than the occasion demanded

have never been in an occasion
which demanded more than me

I have never had the mind's argument
dislodged by the horses of the heart

have never ridden horses
which did not know their riders

I have never risen above
the immediate moment

have never had a moment
which demanded my immediate presence

I have never needed a new face
to meet the faces of my friends

have never had friends with faces
that did not smile back at me.

HERE IT IS SPRING AGAIN

and sorrow in this eager air
has the sudden smell of stones
washed by man-walked streams

certain cotton charms
and the green round of her arm
proclaim the dull return of spring.

Each different-same day the sea
washes its smells on the sands
and a constant tree stands

to be seen every day. Every night
the distraught drum beats
the rhythm of some ancient heart.

Each night the flesh moves
its heavy weight on the air
and at morning the distant

wall of a broken barn breaks
through the nightlong snow.
And with all there is perhaps

a lip to be watered, a clock
to be wound, windows to be opened,
every day in this world that I am.

UNDER THE BO-TREE

for Gilbert Neiman

It is said:
Ants formed an anthill round his head
White loads fell from the sky on his winter body
Yellow leaves spread sunfull desires on his skin
A green arm descended branchlike to earth
With a novel darkness on his eyes.

And the Bo-tree rustled a leaf of sound
And said: This love, this incident will repeat
For other men and other trees. Why, my friend,
For Time will end us out?

And he:
Not against time
For I contain that within this beaten body
And the green that shouts your shoots
Through this flesh and bone
I am the man tomorrow and you
Are the tree

Not against the white horse
That drops from above the sky
Not against the sea that swells
Around my eye
Not a struggle this.

No conspiracy this that rustles your leaf
Trembles this body of mine
The green arm will swell again
And white will be the white-long snow
No, not an unbeing this.

The bird is not deaf
And the ugly man loves
The mirror's reciprocal thought

Stones know their waters too,
No, not a silence this
But a light within my head that resolves
Its painful geometry for you.

LEGEND

Never have eight daughters, says an Indian proverb,
for they may all be barren.

Then the grandmother said,
'I want a grandchild...'
As the night seeks the day
And the tree shouts a sprout

Everything reclaims a birth
To seek a meaning for its death
So the grandmother said
She wanted a grandchild.

'These breasts are the snow
From which no water flows
Between our thighs are stones
Our belly, an empty white cloud'

Said the eight daughters
Of the dying grandmother
Like trees in the yard
On which no bird sits.

'I have killed my father
And struck my mother down
I have stood all alone
Like a cloud in the sky

But my breasts were flowers
And my thighs the roof
Of this world, my belly
Ripe as summer trees

Eight stitches have ruined my life
Eight times these lips have fallen
Have I lived these eighty years
To see but eight stones in my yard?'

The dying woman asked
And like trees
They stood and waited
For the rain to fall.

THE MAN WHO DIED OF A FEVER

Faith moves mountains, they said
and put a book of prayer
beneath his head.
But the fever was stronger

and burnt a yellow hole in the page.
Let the Angels guide him, they said,
and they opened the windows wide
but the sunlight shrank on the floor

and the fever stood like night
beside the sheets of his bed.

And when at last he lay dead
they looked sadly at his bed.
'It must be so,' one shook his head,
'for his soul was dark as lead.'

STILL LIFE

for Constantin Brancusi

Break the air
like a bird

into indivisible planes
indefinable blue
at night, bronze
by day

Moving finer particles
of lighter light proving
that in stillness is motion
most beautiful

Bird of freedom, heaving
oceans in the air, fixed
in flight to a base of bronze,
bronze bird of Brancusi

Move,
move in beauty
and a brown silence over all.

PASTORALE

for Paul Klee

Green
stretched
  the ground
Till
the first broken wall of a barn
broke the rhythm that monotony
sometimes has on the moving eye.

And farther beyond
the barren cypresses
stood like planted arms.

Above all he was
the other one.

Reaching for the river's
brown muscle he found
a single fish moving
like a black arrow.

Bones and distances
were what he sought.

Confined in his cell
he thought
what a wonderful thing it is
that a painting has walls.

And so in secret script
he converged the terror
of the moment lost in space.

Searching for the earth's green root
he found consciousness reflecting
beneath the body's mask.

YELLOW AND BLUE

for Jamini Roy

Yellow and blue
is a way of flight.
The apple is true
and her arm a night
long sadness. Her eye
a white fish of form
and her lip a lie
that the worm

forgot to chew;
for the apple became
an egg and the two
eyes the same.

Yellow and blue
is a colourless silence.
The bird is new
and the brown fence
does not surround
her fish-white eye.
The green round
of her thigh
breaks on the yellow
of the egg as it must
the earth being slow
in turning to dust.

THE BLUE WOMAN

for Jamini Roy

On my wall in my room
is a blue woman whom
I have fixed in the midst
of a dance

fish for eyes and her hands
painted red (for in my country
they like the colour) her feet
big and weighted by metal rings

Her lips lowered in all modesty
a white ring in the only showing
ear, a yellow dress which is all about.
Naked yet, and shy.

But after sleep and after day
when the moon is quiet and dark
and my mind full of walls
my head full of white

is it the blue woman awake?
Her silence released and all around
her movement subtle and her smile
within my closed eyes

Is it the wall, the woman
or the inclosed smile?

FOR ANOTHER NEW YEAR

for Christopher Sripada

Remember how one day, waking
At the neutral hour of evenings brushed over
With hasty forget, with cords of flesh stretching
Between us, mirrors of mutual ruin;

Sharing not only the pain but the blooded joy
In the parented tear-eye of a lost father
Speaking also in language's vulgar overtones
Brushing the sea's hairy face with misty hands

With a subtle grace while you stole the smile
From my lip, and an anxious ear drooped
To lift skyward words dropped in abandon

We, the double-man, I the single lie
And in the nuptial bed, a secret lost.

When the dog's tongue gave a final twist
And the man's thigh slipped away at last
When the moon and the sea lay still over one another
Then, when it was not right, I had thoughts of you.

PORTRAIT OF A MISTRESS

This paper lip that I kiss
Had a life yesterday: opening
Before blackened teeth of bliss
And a smell of early morning.

This silent eye I now deceive
Had a trust yesterday: discovered
In the burning thirst of a sieve
And the empty arms of a beloved.

This empty bed that I press
Holds a summer arm: guilty
Like the falsehoods I profess
And your heaviness in my body.

TO A CHRISTIAN LADY

for Gertrude Wickard

Your flowers, madame,
Oldened, withered by hand,
And impaled on cotton dressed wire

Lead a life wholly new
To their original seed.

Are grateful perhaps, for the frills
You curve them into and the metal
Vases which gild your room.

For flowers are born to die early
Unless watered by your spinster destiny!

Or do your clotted fingers feel the pain
Of roses separated from their thorns
So that younger hands in farther carriages
(in places like China perhaps…)
Can smell through their perfumed noses
Your intricate nosegay
While you recover from beneath
A mildewed skin, a rose once wedded
To the inevitable thorn.

FOR A NUN IN A WAITING ROOM

Her knotted fingers can
not untie the knots she
made yesterday…
All her life, her day, her night
safeguarded within these knots
which she cannot now unknot.

Poor sister, why do I pity you?
Removed on this wooden bench
by bones and distances and
the fears of my eyes,
Shall I help you untie these knots?

Long ago my mother used to make
them too, and eventually I
had to loosen them for her. Old
women's fingers have a habit
of getting that way about such things;
and I have learnt to undo these
little complicacies.

Only will you not let me sit
awhile and watch
your fingers while they fumble
and your rose-red lips
while they mumble.

THE WIDOW IN WASHINGTON SQUARE

Picking her true path
past rainwalked streets
through the russet
of the evening's fade

flares of jaded grass
in her eyes and the
slow-dying dreams of
her many loves

the widow walks through
Washington Square.

Many rains have fallen
on the many stones
laid like graves
on the street

Many women have leaned
out of the window's shade
to shout to the many
children in the streets

Many lovers have walked
their repeated agonies
many days and many nights
have sunk their teeth

in the smoke from the many
chimneys. Yet today
was a different day.
It has been colder before

and warmer suns have shone
on the square, colder
partings have seared her heart.

Yet today, as every day
sadder than yesterday
the widow walks through
Washington Square.

THE PETER GRIMES OF BENJAMIN BRITTEN

There is the ringing of a bell somewhere
Said the fisherman
And a weaving of the nets of night in my skull

Remoteness by rain or riverache
Unapproached by fish or foam
There is the love of child
Or surfbreaks within my heart

Cannonade of conversations by wailmouth
Rockhungry ocean's raucologues

Line, prolong your agony
Sound, beat an inaccessible walk
On the seabed of memory
Eyes escape that tideless point

In the brain
White or withered by moon

Sunshine and seamstress tremble
In the tortured nest of night
Seaweed and decaying lips must
Return to the original womb.

SOMETIMES

Sometimes it is the tragedy of words and meanings
Sometimes of ambitions and fulfillments
Sometimes it is the nameless fear at the base of your skull.

Sometimes it is the private pain of love
Living under the surface like an unhealed wound.
Sometimes it is the distortion of your face
In a cracked mirror.
The unrecorded thoughts, the unregistered feeling.

Sometimes it is the hushed light
The coarse fingers, the vulgar breasts
The reek of beer, the dimensionless smoke
And the Saturday night receding.

Sometimes it is the solitary lamp post
And the little fingers of rain
Knocking on the window pane
The loneliness of your room
And the empty bed.

VALDSTEJNSKA HOSPADA, PRAHA

Looking at her face
One would have thought,
And I did,

She is maybe Gertrude Stein
Or Marianne Moore in her
Stupid hat or the other one
Who'd burnt her candle

At both ends. An old face
With young mischievous eyes
A red blouse and a stark
Black suit. A magazine

Of the arts in her hand,
Alone at a table with a basket
Of bread and a goblet
Of red Viennese wine.

A once-upon-a-time lesbian
And now in need
Of a man to tell her
That the paintings she'd buy
On Sunday afternoon auctions
And the poets she'd propagate
On her Wednesday evenings
Were all without meaning

A man to rough her up a bit
With his coarse lips
And his unshaved-on-Sunday face
To light the candle

She'd been holding these many years
Unlit among the books and
Paintings and schoolgirls
Trying to learn the piano.

A TASTE FOR DEATH

Shared we such a room
on Sherman Street, only
this is Washingtonova
and several years dead now

I open the closet and find
bottles of wine, poems
on my typewriter and stories
on yours, rejection slips

and cigarette stubs on the parquette floor
a Klee on the wall for me
and a Patchen for you, Old
Bunk Johnson shuffling by Mozart.

Such was our life, twin-bedded
jealous of the one and in love
with the other, a passion for apple-pie
or a taste for Death.

Only dead now, these several years
your self turns up to meet me
on these stone-paved streets
and I cannot remember your eyes.

Shall we say, Christoph,
the pact is ended
and I cannot turn a sudden tear
for the memory of your love.

Your life was full of body
frail but full of flesh, bursting
like an apple on the table
keen to be killed.

MARRIED LOVE

Every evening
I am met at the gate by my wife
her hair in disorder and her dress a mess
from the kitchen
and the girls hang on the leaves of the gate
while my ancient car rolls in.
One carries my bag, the other
my lunch basket
the day's work is over and I am home.
I have forgotten them all day and now
suddenly remember that I must
disappoint them again
for my evening is planned
for a meaningless excursion to the bars.
And the coffee which my wife has served
is cold in my mouth
and the tales the children have brought from school
are dull on my ears.
In spite of my love for them
I must disappoint them again tonight.

MIDDLE AGE

When the skin has stretched tighter
on the bones of the face
and the face closer shaved
with distinctive moles and warts
When lips have softened with love
and the eyes hardened with age
and the stomach achieved
a wholesome round
and the legs move with a known swagger
When a life is half over
and Death is yet to be
and beauty no longer of the body

Oh to be middle-aged
and competent
and moneyed and loved
among other things
Husband and father
Friend and inadequate lover!

I LIKE THE AMERICAN FACE

I like the American face
successful, clean shaven
closely clothed
with arrogance of chin
but soft of eye
and always ready
to break into a false-toothed smile

The kind of face
that photographs so well in *Time*
a face with the races so well mixed
yet wholly new
and all American
as apple-pie

Individually interesting
but pointless on the whole
sexless on the surface
with a hint of pleasures
beneath the skin
carefully controlled
by the waist-band

Successful as I said
in the jut of lip
and the tooth's proclamation
of the body's supremacy
over the mind.

GONE NOW

They are all gone
Gone is the googly bowler
And the getter of runs
The cutter of stones
And the maker of words
Each has gone
And left a void
In my world of wood
But the lessons of the one

are not good for the other
And if you live a full life
By which I mean, raise
A family, love a wife
And generally be
What is there to fear of Death
Which is but a mere cease
Of a heartbeat
The sudden stoppage of Is.

I SIT HERE

I sit here
in my loneliness
alternating
between the book
of Modern Verse
and the Return of the Hood
Unable to gain satisfaction
from Swinburne or Spillane

The transistor on the table
provides
the right amount of noise
and my daylight tube light
made by Philips India
illuminates the right areas

But my mind flies
to Paramaribo and Dakar
on the radio dial

places of pleasure
peopled with laughter

And my eyes fix themselves
on images of beauty
that I'll never see
beyond this well
of my loneliness.

LIFE HAS BEEN

Mostly
a matter of living these days
Simply
a subject of the senses
surrounding this body
Really
repeating the words of others
and doing the deeds
of those that have done them already
Merely
a matter of the moment
within the hand.

And yet
occasionally
out of hand
inexplicable
a moment of time
that is beautiful
or sad
a breath of splendour

a flicker of greatness
that keeps one going
for the million other hours
in a life
that has been
mostly a matter
of living the days.

THESE DAYS

My pen is so heavy
It hardly crawls on the page
Dragging a chain of hesitant words
Trying to give meaning to what is not there.
These days

So much of me is submerged
In this act of living
Raising a family, loving a wife
In meaningless conversations with friends
Or simply sitting on the grass
Vacant of mind

That I wonder now
Where was the fire that burnt me
Where the words that danced on the periphery
Eluding my reach with their many moods
And where the man within
Who searched the streets for love
And where was the arm that betrayed me
With its tenderness.

AN ORDINARY LIFE

The first decade had best be left unremembered
With kisses, pattings and beatings
None of which I could really comprehend
A child among others with no mind of my own

In my twenties I was in love
With books, paintings and music
And similar passions;
Women lurked in the corners of my mind

In my thirties they warmed my bed
Displaced friends, found fault
With me when I did not always comply
With their demands on my time and money

In my forties they lost interest in me
Children were more important
And when the problems of Life
Loomed large, liquor helped me sleep

In my fifties, first it was an ulcer
And then my heartbeats got awry
Unwise indulgences had begun
The decay of my body and soul

In my sixties, I tried to find peace
But my mind would fly in myriad ways
Regretting past mistakes
And making new resolutions that couldn't be kept

Friends made way to companions
Sons and daughters crossed my path

Grandchildren would play with me
As with a toy that often went out of order

Here now, on the verge of seventy
Unsatisfactory husband, irate father
Ugly, old, much misunderstood man
I begin to philosophise on my failures

And sprout platitudes
That have lost all meaning
On a life that is almost over
With too little to show

10 DOWNING STREET

I saw a few books in a pub
the other day
calico-bound volumes on a mahogany shelf
over a marble mantelpiece

10 Downing Street it's called
with a picture of Churchill
proudly displayed
over the bound books

A pitcher of beer and some crisps later
I walk over to see the titles
of the attractive books
unimaginative titles by
nondescript authors
that you'd find in British clubs

of the old Cantonment days
or in P & O liners on the high seas

but there's a volume of Cyril Connolly
to surprise me, and a few poems by
second rate poets, for a change
2000 watts of power beats the music
of today flickering between the lights
to drown out the frail voice
of a Swedish singer

which surfaces now and then by intent

Is this the India that I have come back to?
– tempted by Gandhi's gospel and Nehru's call
after centuries of slavery. Have we come to this?
Bound by the shackles that we overthrew not so long ago.

THE GOLDEN GATE

Dear Jag:
Just to tell you of my latest bug
The Golden Gate
By Vikram Seth
A fellow Stanfordian who does us proud
For the likes of us who are still around
That were part of the still familiar scene
Berkeley to Stanford and all that lay in between
And wanted to do it but didn't
Plain fact was perhaps we just couldn't
With Phil and Ed, June and Jane
And that wily li'l old Charlemagne.

Here's a book that I strongly recommend
For all Indo-Anglians that are trying to vend
Their latest versions of our Great Culture
For the Western Vultures
And like most of our time
Indians do well in a foreign clime
How I dread to think of Vikram's fate
If he'd stayed behind in his native State
And tried to produce a similar Tome
Of similar happenings here at home.

SOME THOUGHTS ON TREES

Trees have no overcoats to protect them

and simply die
in the winter
as well as they are born
each succeeding spring

man has machines
to comfort his body
and condition his mind

trees have no overcoats to shed
so much to put on and so much to cast aside
ridiculous in either costume
and uneasy without

the hard core of man is as of the tree
with its dead branches in the winter weirdness
and a leaf-left frailty of autumn

or the green bud that plunges its root in spring
and the yellow proclamations of flower
leaves and other summer splendours

There is a tree within me

that shoots its green barbs
through this bark of flesh and bone

that shouts its raw-red sprouts
through these coats of skin

that breaks its sore points
on these eyes of water

that speaks its hungers
through these veins of mine

that wreaks its vertical agony
through the surge of blood in my groin

They have written on leaves before

but what a conspiracy this
between that tree without

my window and the willing
within this body here

white loads have fallen from the sky
and my wishes are winter men

yellow leaves have spread
...

PICTURES AT AN EXHIBITION

Words do not like music move
nor like a picture play upon the senses
Here mostly
it is a matter of silences
within the self
the slow travail of thoughts
that stick in the throat

And how often has my poor medium
betrayed me
in the middle of a mood
by the paucity of its power
And how often have I held myself
at a tremble
on the threshold of a discovery
that this word could not contain

Picasso is passé
and Miro is no more
Yet one stands transfixed
at the sight of what
one need not understand
the shapes and colours
that speak the inexplicable
unlike the word

Yes,
I trade in a different medium
my goods are not for ready sale
I have nothing to state
that will startle your senses
If I am vague, oh do not ask –

and if my meanings are clear
please do not step over me too quickly

YOU CAN DIE

crossing the street
or be
the sole survivor of a ship sunk at sea.

It is all a matter of choice
not yours.

But whether you wish
to look at flowers

or bury your children
in the backyard

it is of your own making
Whether of the mind

or because the body's horse
leaps through your eye

It is all because
of the way you are shaped
to be the present horror
in your mirror

THE DEAD

We love the dead
For their being so

Stowed away in the solitary
Seclusion of the individual mind.

Avoidable as necessary,
Available at a moment's recall

To fill the tears in a drawing-room
Many years later.

THIS IS JUST TO SAY

I do not grieve every time
There is a death in the street
But a man died today
Whom I last saw placing a rose
In his button-hole.

The rose has now left the rose tree
Rootless amidst the thorn
And the garden has ruined the gardener.
Graves will not remember him
For his dust has joined the earth's dust
And flowers will forget that his face
Was ever a full-blown flower.

This was a man whose life has filled my life
This was a man whose death will diminish me.

I DO NOT GRIEVE EVERY TIME

there is a death in the world
but today
a girl died whom
I last saw
picking flowers with a thin
smile on her face

Now sorrow sits thinly on my own
though I have seen its various shapes
cloud my heart like a sudden shadow

The death of a dog beneath the wheels
of an express train
someone dead on the street and the living
collecting coins on his body

The death of someone not seen but heard
in the next room
suddenly stopping the heart

My own with its bewildering terrors
its agonising questions and the
answers from the seashore

The death of loved ones never properly expressed
and the death on the wide screen with its
tensions magnified, stretching the sentiments
on a violin concerted in beauty

'Oh do not let the dead live beyond their life
Let not cold tears fall on the warm flesh
And your tears disturb the world in laughter.'

But yesterday a girl died whom I see today
picking flowers with laughter in her body
and no death in her eyes.

A FUNERAL

Tell me you people
who are gathered here
with your apt faces
and your broad shoulders

Are tears
so
necessary

Is my face
fitted for
the occasion,
does
sorrow
sit well on me?

Tell me for I face it
alone
without mirrors.
Would you have me show
a stout heart
or rather see me
break down in tears?

Are you here
because they say

if you do not see him
to the grave no one will
see you to yours?

Tell me you people
who are gathered here
to share my sorrow.

And does it not
matter, my people,
for you to know,
for instance,

If I loved him
with my heart
or used my mind for
the daily intercourse

If his physical absence
felt like his physical presence
tell me my people
for you are here
to share my suffering.

Can you feel the pain in my fingers
as they grope for yours? Can you see
what my eyes cannot see
that I wish to be alone
rather that I did not
have to have loved or
suffered as you you'd have me

Or for that matter
to have to be here

Tell me you people
who are here
to bare your bosom
and cover me with the
silence
of your non-sorrow.

I AM ALL THAT I LOVE

I am all that I love
if for an instant's being

Yes doctor, I am you too
and at 66 your hair
floats like thistle into my mind
every graying weed
has a root in me.

And you too Christoph, I am you
if only in the jaded flares
of your quick-passioned heart
How many tangled ways have
crossed us by?

And you, absent one,
I am you too and the bones
and distances you carried within,

If all the pains you have caused
leaped like gravestones
all the corpses would be me.

For I am all that I love!

But of course, dear mother, I
almost forgot, I never could
tell you the love I feel for you

You know, love
is such a funny thing when you
feel it most you least can tell

To you, I shall give me
without subtraction
For you never wanted
what you most gave

I am all that I am that I love,
Well, yes, of course…

SUNRISE OVER KAMAREDDY

Sunrise would not be sunrise
nor would the sun set over the hills
if it were not for you being here

Otherwise
the fact without feeling would not
be an occurrence like any other.

The sun sets or rises
in my heart that is full of you
and the river sad, the mountain forlorn
I am not I without you

and my body exists like a bone
feeding for itself
without the feeling heart
or the seeing eye

or the sadness that is all around me here
and nowhere else
but in the cold rise of the sun
over the December lake

through a mist of memory
to keep me alive
for you that are not here.

ALL KINDS OF LOVE

Yes,

I have this thing about them
Gross of body, florid of face
Full lipped and wild haired
Fat old men with flat white faces
That shine out of the pages of *Time*
And speak to me

Of the unspeakable pleasures possible
Between our bodies.

Beneath every rape
There is hope
For peace with the flesh
And before my body is taken

My mind has fallen
As I await my special doom
Knowing that some day
The commerce of our bodies
Will end
In the meeting of our minds

And that tenderness will travel
From his arm to mine.

FOR MULK RAJ ANAND

You have similarities
with Picasso:
I mean in the ugliness
of your bare body

For was it not he
that showed us beauty
in ugliness.

Bare of body
with a woman's flabby breasts
and sensuous folds of flesh

Your ravaged face
and luminous eyes
burn into me
from the page.

What I mean is,
You hold a fascination for me

wholly physical
and your body seeks my betrayal.
But it is just another way
to say
that our minds have met
a long while ago

and your words have stripped
my soul naked
as I now lust
for your body that breaks
in black and white
upon my hungry eyes.

NAGARJUNAKONDA

And you my father
who did not let me see you then
now face me in your old age
as I feed you with my hands.
Love and pity will not explain
the hurt of my then young pain
and what I feel for you now
is but a token of thanks
for your sperm that gave me root

You my father
that gave me being
can you see me now
as you were then –
strong as these stones?
Or do your tired eyes

see in me the vision of your broken dreams
as I counter my impotence
with your infallibility?

And you old man
hungry yet for the pleasures of life
lean thy strong body
on my frail arm,
and lust for the world
while I face the shame
of being thy son
full of the love that I cannot share with you.

POEM

In India
Women

Have a way
Of growing old

My mother
For instance

Sat on the floor
A hundred years

Stirring soup
In a sauce-pan

Sometimes staring
At the bitter neem tree in the yard

For a hundred years
Within the kitchen walls.

GODHULI TIME

It is the cow-dust hour
And smoke lies heavy over my head
As I walk across these earthen paths
And smells of burnt milk from inside
Mingle with those from the fields outside

I turn a corner
And surprise a pair
Besides the haystacks
Whispering sweet everythings.
She smiles and flies
Like a bird, her anklets
Ringing, her mirror-work skirt in a flutter
While he plucks a strand of hay
Foolishly from a corner of his teeth.

It is Godhuli time
And darkness is but a few minutes away
Man and bird and beast
Turn towards the flickering lights
That beckon them home
And in the distance I can see
The lighted windows of a fleeting train
That has brought me here

While my thoughts travel towards
The home that I have never had.

DIWALI DAYS

These two
sit in the house,
hardly a word
between them.
One is hard
of hearing
and a cataract
makes it difficult
for the other
to see.

Shaking like
leaves on the tree
waiting to drop,
my father and mother,
for we have left them

And at festival time
they gather,
the sons and daughters,
grandchildren and in-laws.
And while the women
serve and scramble around
the men sit on the floor
for the annual meal.
We have no words
for each other

except for pleasantries
and share the common guilt
while the children cackle
and sometimes fight.

But my father and mother,
their hearts are full
and their eyes flood with tears
as they see their children
and their children's children
The mango tree in the yard
is full of birds again

But at eventide
each of us leaves
with the usual words
of farewell,
and the hearts full
of emptiness.
For tomorrow is another day
and the old people
are left again
with each other
to look at the walls
and the pictures
on the walls.

MY SON

I have this only child
after these many years
alone with my husband.

Looking at the men around me
I have often wanted a son
like them

My brother
My lover
My husband

But this boy
is so like me
that I am afraid

the world's wave
will topple him
and this love

that I flood him with
will surely be understood
as but a sign of my shame.

FRIENDSHIP

When old friends meet
out of school
and have nothing to remember
but the borrowed copy-book

and the school gym
where love hung
on the handle-bars
and the time has now come
to talk of wives unseen
and children only heard
and love no longer free
for distribution.

When lonely roads are walked
in each other's company
muted by the years between
remembering now
what has been long forgotten
and suddenly called
into the memory
by a chance encounter
at the crossroads
of a foreign city.

ON APPROACHING FIFTY

I have come a way now
and the meanings of life
are clearer to me.

I have read a little
seen somewhat
tasted a bit

of everything. But
there is nothing I know
really

Full circle
I am back
at the beginning

but without the wonder
of being a child again.

SHAKUNTALA

Shakuntala, Shakuntala
the beautiful daughter
of the famous sage
went with loving heart
to the palace of the Iron King

On the way she sang
to her maidens
Walk slowly walk softly
We must be sure
my Lord will be home
when we are come...

Shakuntala, Shakuntala
Oh my daughter
of the wasp-black hair
and the fish-white eye
Oh my daughter
for the king has forgotten you

Walk slowly
through the green
walk softly
over the brown

So long ago
Oh my daughter
The hunt is now over
And the doe's eye wet
beneath the grass
Those were thorns
that were his body
That was a lie
your body softened for
Oh my daughter
For the king has forgotten you…

And the king
he sat in his chamber
weaving cords of forget –
The hut of woven grass
and the frightened deer
he had saved
for your love…

They were not in his eye, my daughter
They were not in his eye

For He sits on an Iron Throne
And all around him are iron walls.

And his men
they took his message
and a pot of honey

for the little boy
which meant
he did not desire her.

Oh my daughter
For the king has forgotten you...

Shakuntala, Shakuntala
the beautiful daughter
of the famous sage
returned sadly
to the forest

And on the way
her maidens sang
Walk slowly
through the green
Walk softly
over the brown.

STREETS

I have walked these old familiar streets
many a time
as a child and a boy, young man, and now not yet old
I make these right-angled turns
with the street dogs smelling each other and the old
bungalows now bricked up into blocks
for brothers or tenants
and the architecture of red and white iron grilles
replaces the weary mango trees and the coconut palms

Nothing remains for me here
except the shouts of children
or the bark of a somewhere chained dog
The old familiar faces have gone underground
submerged in their strife
And all I have is a memory of the old days
when as kids we shouted across the compound walls
or as young men lit the nights with our drunken songs
and raced these streets with the silencers off
on our OK Supremes
Nothing remains now
except these neat back streets that turn away
as I approach them.

OLD RAIN

Am I your lost past?
For heaven's sake stop
Treating me like a child
The golden boy you were once
That tomorrow will be you or you or you
To fit me into the pattern
Of growth or decay
That others clothed you in before
So that you can say
It had to come to this.

You wait, soon
I'll be forty
And I'll say
(but what an incomplete triumph
for you my mockers will all be dead)

'Well, here now, I am forty
And I haven't seen or known
What you would have me see
What you would have me know.
These eyes have seen, this body
thrilled or suffered alternately
Night has filled my body
And I have filled my weight on the day
I have known the thousand treacheries
I have felt the death of the heart
I have gone through all.'

And before me will be a circle of eyes
(As ours are before you now)
Then will I pick the bluest eye of all
And I will say to her:
(Sadly, wistfully, though
That is the only way to revoke desire,
Your past face from the present face)
Then I will say to her:
'You my dear are far too young
Wait till you are as old as me.'

Then will I tell her
Of the roots that will harden within
Or the blood that will flow slower with reason
Of the desires that will invade
Her mind and her body
To make her into the present ruin that you are.
And while she steps from stage to stage
(and the desert feet are not alone)
Then will I be the insistent voice
The voice before and
The voice after

That will say:
'Nothing is new, I
Have been there, your
Pain and your pleasure
Look in the mirror
You'll find a thousand similar.'

FOR JOHN EVERYMAN, POET

Nobody thought
this was how poor John would go
One friend at the funeral was heard
Making the remark
'All these thirty years
I'd never known it'd be so.'

Was one, I'm told, much given to silence
and drunken gusts of brilliant talk
Had a number of friends, poets, painters
and people of the streets as he'd say
Had on occasion been seen at the galleries
with the wife of Consolidated Chemicals.

Adolescence, my boy, is a funny thing.
I was in Paris, penniless, didn't own a thing
And what a time we had of it
'Paris is so prone to pornography'
was his favorite saying.

At thirty his voice was milder
and the critics said marriage
has mellowed his taste. 'Best

love poetry since Donne'
raved one.

And to the Museum of Arts
they drove in herds
to hear him recite
his latest verse.

In his fortieth year he started to write
his autobiography. Friends said it was right
he should be the one
to record their fun.
'All my friends are geniuses' he began
That year they predicted he'd be
in the Yeats anthology.

Fifty years closed round him a new
fear, but not of death.
'You know my friends,' he'd say
'I've had visions too.
Someday emerging at last
from this terrifying vision
I must write or I'll burst,
Lord give me time,' he'd pray.

This was his major work
'Explorations' he called it
No one showed jealousy or surprise
when he was awarded the coveted prize
'The very best, this side
of the ocean,' they cried.

Twenty-four hours later, they
found him in his room, quite dead

with a bullet in his head.
Must be cancer they said,
Poor fellow, couldn't bear to tell Jo…

THIS POEM

I speak not of the mystery that is woman
Nor of the great white being that is God –
I do not speak of love, or of people,
For I have known neither father nor lover
And none have I reached with what I cannot utter.

But I speak of the lonely word
That will not reach beyond my tongue
Nor fulfill my frustrations.

There are things beyond this word.
I know –

That the grocer's bill and the rising
Prices occupy me most,
Concern my body with their ignominy
Break my will with their boundary
Reduce my rest and snatch the spoken thought
Before it can find the page.

This too I know, that love is
All, that truth and beauty and
The standard values of an ordered mind
Are what remains behind my bone.

By my lonely soul I will only see
The beauty of an orange on a table
Or a word in a poem.

TO AN EDITOR

You ask me for a poem
And I say
I have them in hundreds
Not written.

The bird in the air
Or a leaf on the tree
Love in the throat
Or the Lion's leap in the dark –

These are all poems,
In a way.

The rhythm is in the motion or the stillness
The reason in the word or the silence.
But the body which has given these shelter
The forest, the concrete tree, the suspect sky –

These have roots within the consciousness
and expressed
altogether otherwise
than what you'd say is a poem.

YESTERDAY

In the bus
on the way
to Los Angeles

An old man
was the only
one who sat
beside me

Other men and
other women stood
with blank eyes
and unlovely faces

but this old man
with beautiful eyes
sat beside me

This beautiful blind man
beside an old nigger woman.

IT RAINS SOFTLY ON THE CITY

Rimbaud

Wormwood and water return
the smell of morning
mildew of memory and the fresh
spider stain on the roses
in the drawing room
do not relieve

the recurring monotony
of days hung like wax
on the skin of my life

But I:
inside myself there is a world
where the moon becomes
the empty hollow of a spoon
and the sky a blue sufficiency
in the wink-less eye
and the sun a turn
from dark to light
from the mind's tight
to the unclosing, soft-circled…
'Lightning does not break
the thunder's absolute vigil
The nightingale does not
approach the soft end of day
The sea does not recede
where the sands concede

Inside,
              inside yourself,
                                          there is a world

subject to the many excursions
of my soul'

Said the rain
softly in the city.

OPENING DAY... UNIVERSITY OF CALIFORNIA

... and yesterday
The mighty womb threw open its iron portals
intending, perhaps, to release the floods...
But more and more poured in,
not the seers but the seekers:
each with separate intent
deliberate, bold, and
in private pursuit
of the common fruit.

The while,
amidst the bookstore bickerings,
the shuffling feet and the painted veils
I lay beneath
like a broken bow
wearied, and, of a sudden, old.

In the sky, a trail of smoke read
Burmah-Shell or some such...
But all I saw,
a million questions and a million un-answers;
octopus-feet and scorpion-tails in succession
ravaged the vistas of my mind:
deserts in aery suspension and dried-up oases.

And, below, on our floor
automobiles crept,
men and women like innumerable larvae
scuttled.

And in the blue beyond
the hoary Rockies squatted like Indian cows;

and the river flowed in lazy ecstasy;
and the fish in denuded delight
courted with quivering gills.

While we, poor humans,
in civilized counterfeit
moved and moved.

And so the record changes
and plays again – single-paged truths
documented, catalogued and preserved.

And when my voice is a silence, huge as the earth
the ricochet speaks.

PORTRAITS OF AMERICA

Snow 1

The snow lies
on the rail
like a broken snake

It climbs this branch
and down another
it falls on the leaves

accumulated
like a fine white rain.

Snow 2

Atop
the wood-green
shingle porch
projecting
from brick-red
brick walls
the snow sat
all of twenty
four hours.

Capitol Building

At night
the Capitol

Building
shines

like an embalmed corpse

being the effect
of subdued lights

Sherman Street runs
into the capitol steps

and to the right
are Democrat dining halls

and to the left
Republican restrooms

on either side
of the capitol building.

Department store window

He had seen them swinging
in his amorphous gaze
behind the glass and gold
of a noonday window

the smells embracing his eyes
and the novel desires revealing
in the near-dark nates of his wife
receding into the corner of the kitchen

Had brought it home to secrete his desires
within the pneumatic satisfactions
of a rose he had never lipped.

Apartment house

In spite of
three great
big windows

at ten o'clock
my room
is dark

You can do
nothing
about such things.

If the sun rises
in the east
three big windows

in the west
are no help at all
at ten in the morning

The Mother

Her nipples have
widened from
original points

into black diaphragms
open to hands and
the spread of weather

Her desire has split
from man to child.

The Park

Two bronze seals

in the waterless oval
of the park, ply
their constant trade

balancing imaginary balls
on their noses
each supporting
a black boy

on their back

And on circular rows of green
benches, browned by bird shit
and rain, old men sit and stare
pants worn, souls torn
each wholly alone
in his observation
of the unhappy seals.

Used cars

The number of
used car lots

all by the
main street

convinces me
that the men
in this city
are a dissatisfied bunch.

Snow 3

How pure the snow
as it falls fresh

onto my black overcoat
from a blue sky

covers the green beds
and escapes the metal pavement.

How like white
is the white snow

Before tomorrow's sun
takes it all away

and leaves the streets
brown as before.

Snow 4

White loads
have fallen
from the sky
And the trees
let down
destructive arms
yellow leaves
have spattered
on the green
green beds.
The little cone tree
sits forlorn
like a dog
in the rain.

TRANSLATIONS

Arudra (Bhagavatula Sankara Sastri, 1925–98)

THE TRAIN YOU WOULD WISH TO TAKE

The train you would wish to take
Is forever a lifetime too late
And bored with the wait you board
Any old train that comes your way
The weight of your ideals that you drag
Behind you is far in excess of what
The rules permit, and I am afraid
You'll have to leave your laden heart
In the brake-van of your dreams:
There is no room for all that you've brought
For you can't take it with you, and before
You're hardly in it, the train
Has moved away.

This train will not take you for sure
To the place you would wish to reach
So, why not blame the Gods
And stay right where you are.

Sri Sri (Srirangam Srinivasa Rao, 1910–83)

A POEM

Squarely, solid
In the city square
The bull sat
All of a lifetime.
A generation ago
And the generation after
The river's muscle

Flowed
Uninterrupted
But for this moment
This stone-eyed bull
This king for a day
Silent as the wash
Of white on the wall
Ignoring equally
The motor horn of man
And the longer arm
Of the punisher
Complacent, non-violent
Concupiscent, totally teetotal
Squarely, solid
In the city square.

SAD VOICES

What shall we tell you
Why we are weeping
We do not know
Why we are weeping
You ask us for a meaning
Well we know nothing
Who? Why? What?
We do not know anything
When? Where? Why?
What questions are these that you ask?

Ask the throatless wind
Or the spread sky
Yes, it's a terrible thing
What was not expected has come to be

Do you still ask
Why we are weeping
Not one or two
Not a family or a tree or a town
Not a country or a subcontinent
But the whole world today
Is submerged in this sorrow
This is an international tragedy
On a CinemaScope scale
The Jew in Wall Street
And the African black
The king in his palace
And the coolie in his factory
Not one or two
Not a hundred or a thousand
But from this end to the other
The world
Is engrossed in this evil.

Do you still ask?
Shall I continue.............?

Sishtla (Uma-Maheswara Rao, 1909–53?)

CALL ME BY A NAME

Call me by a name
A rose if you will
For my trite story
Has all the sadness
Of that flower.

Alone now, a grief after
In memory of that golden boy
And pierced by the eyes of these women
I sit now and remember
The mountain slopes where his green smile
Took me and left me in the mud brown day.

Alone now, a grief away
From my village
Awake in the afternoon's clutch
I await my death that will not come.

With remembrances of mother, of sisters
Of my father and my brothers, remembrances
Of those that I belonged to, and you
A last remembrance of you that I lost.
Memory of nightfall, of darkness
And of you my sweet-smelling man
My love is true as this memory-ridden night.

Remembrances at daybreak and in the train
Of thoughts in the brain, remembrances at nightfall
In my plundered bed
Remembering you now that winter is here
Remembering you now that spring has come
Remembering you with the rain
Remembering you this second in time
You my broad-shouldered one
Where are you now, lover man?

Sing me a song my sweet-faced sinner
Love me a little my disloyal one
The girls in that town are a-waiting for you

The girls in this town are a-waiting for you
Alone in the afternoon's lap I am for you

Lover, come back to me like my memory of you
Lover, bring back to me what you took of me
Lover, take back from me what you gave me

Come to me, love, in man shape
Break into me, love, in boy shape
Sink into me softly, love, in girl shape.

Hush a bye my baby the birds are about
Softly my child lest the winds hear you
My breasts are rocks, love, waiting for your mouth.

Over the seas I sing you a song
Over the rocks I'll borrow a rhyme
For you, lover,
I will shout my name
Rose, Rose, Rose!

Ajanta (Penumarti Viswanatha Sastri, 1929–98)

NOBODY, NOWHERE

> *'…In the real dark night of the soul it is always three o'clock in the morning…'*
>
> F. SCOTT FITZGERALD

Nobody, nowhere
Silence has fallen on the schoolboy's notebook
And the harlequin wipes the smile from his face
The singer in the street has no more sadness

The woman of joy has closed her door of happiness
In the real dark night of the soul
At three o'clock in the morning
Nobody, nowhere.

The murderer has sheathed his knife
And the queen washes her silken hands
The poor man has hung his tears out to dry
And the prisoner casts a wistful look at the sky
In the real dark night of the soul
At three o'clock in the morning.

Is it the time to look into the mirror?
It is the time to measure the deep?
Is it the time to shut the door of death?
It is the time when the morning opens like a grave?
The beggar in the street and the posters on the wall
Have found their peace
Mr. K ... in his cubicle sleeps
Underneath a robe of thorns
The hearer and the horror have reached their home
Nobody nowhere now
At three o'clock in the morning.

The king and the kingmaker
The common man and the uncommon man
The man of peace and the man of God
Have locked up their miseries
In the safe deposits of their mind.

Nobody nowhere now
Between the murderer and his message
Between the mirror and the ugly man's reciprocal thought
Between this man and that man

There is nobody nowhere now
In the real dark night of the soul
At three o'clock in the morning.

Neither desire nor jealousy
No hope nor despair
Neither sigh nor hate
Disturb the silences of the dark
At three o'clock in the soul.

Tarigonda Venkamamba (1899–1949)
from VISHNUPARIJATAMU
('THE DIVINE FLOWER OF VISHNU')

Gently he lifts me up
Wipes the stream of tears from my eyes
Trails his fingers softly through my twisted hair
Braids my tresses and decks them with flowers
Gently requests that I change my crumpled clothes
Into a flowered raiment of his choice
And adorns me with trinkets of gold and silver.
On my forehead he places the
Vermilion mark of fidelity and artfully
Darkens my reddened eyes with *kaja*!
And on my breasts with his own hands
Playfully rubs a sandal salve to
Cool my burning flesh:
Slowly guides me to his chamber
And cajoles me with
Loving appeals to 'let me know'
The secret reason for my sulk
(As if he didn't know)

And I, like a fool, tell him
About the flower that he
Gave Rukmini, the other one.
Whereupon he laughs lightly,
'Oh that,' he says sweetly,
'To poor Rukmini I have given
A single petal of the Parijat.
To you I'll present the whole
Tree if you wish.
And now come into my arms
I cannot tarry much longer.'
And so again, fool that I am,
I believe the charming rogue
And suffocate him with my kisses.
And as I lie in love-drugged sleep,
He leaves me, as is his wont,
For another bed.
Tell me, my dear, where Tarigonda's Lord is now.
Find him, my dear, the beloved libertine,
And bring him back into my arms.

Tallapragada Viswasundaramma (1899–1949)

JAILHOUSE CLOCK

You need no money
to enter this mighty kingdom
Without a copper coin or measure
to meet your daily needs
You can shed the weight of responsibility
to live your life out here
You need no wage or money
to avail yourself of these services

Everything goes by this clock
that moves with such awesome precision
This magic clock that has no time set
Time in this jail goes on and on.

Nidumanuri Revati Devi (1951–81)

MY STRICKEN VOICE

All these days
While I babbled
Because I had nothing to say
You listened to whatever I said.

And now
Now that I have something to tell you
Something very deep
Something I like
Something pure
When I have something to tell you
And I begin to talk
There is no one to hear
That is why maybe
This voice is now mute
Because of its intoxication perhaps
Or perhaps its sweetness
Or because anyway you
Won't hear it
This voice is stilled.

No matter

In this silenced voice lie
The stirrings of an awakened heart
Buried this long in
Drunken slumber.

EMBERS OF HOPE

Long long after my birth
Realizing I am alive
I feel like weeping for the first time
Because there is no way I can live
Not from a strength of will that takes me beyond pleasure or pain
Nor from a numbness that cannot tell the difference
Nor from an ignorance that cannot distinguish the two.

My life like my birth was uneventful
Unresisted actions in which I was not the subject
Physically, emotionally, morally
I am as responsible for them
As I am for my birth
This awakening sprouting forth suddenly
This moment when I am face to face with myself
From this moment of realization that I am alone
I am responsible for all that I do or leave undone
Some longing, desire, pain
Some confusion agony turmoil
A loneliness an emptiness
Imprisoned by my past
My life is not my own
What if I am born this moment
Break free of all these bonds.

Not that I cannot break them
Nor that I cannot rebel
Nor that I am afraid of the world's stings
Having succumbed to a weakness
I am but the spark of the embers of hope.

PROSE

CITY OF MINE

I love this city and would live nowhere else in this world, but I must concede that this is a mediocre city, a drab town not quite small but not a city at all. Though it has produced a Ramdas Katari and a Sarojini Naidu,[4] its effect on, or its contribution to, the culture of our country have been negligible. When I brought out my *East and West* magazine from this city, the *Bharat Jyoti* gave a glowing review under the title 'A surprise from Secunderabad'. And, in fact, this is generally true of many things. It is of Ramdas Katari, or Ara the painter, or Jaisimha the cricketer, or Jairaj the film star.[5] Brilliance yes, but discovered in other places and yet really 'a Surprise from Secunderabad'. Everything is available in its shops and yet if you must recommend a particular shop to a friend from out of town, you begin to scratch your head. Similarly for a hotel or a cinema or just a place for a good time. Everything and yet nothing! It is a city to stay in and not to visit. Neither a tourist attraction nor a tourist trap. Beautiful girls to catch a glimpse of in speeding cars but not to see on the streets. Lovely buildings, beautiful streets and gardens with flowers

---

4 Admiral Ram Dass Katari (1911–83) was the first Indian to serve as the Chief of Naval Staff. Although born in what is today Tamil Nadu, he grew up in Hyderabad. Poet and nationalist leader Sarojini Naidu (1879–1949) was born in Hyderabad.

5 Both the painter Krishnaji Howlaji Ara (1914–85) and the cricketer Motganhalli Laxminarsu Jaisimha (1939–99) were born in Secunderabad, while the film star, director and producer Paidi Jairaj (1909–2000) was born in Karimnagar, north-east of Hyderabad.

all locked in secrecy within high walls or behind inaccessible driveways.

Take for instance this incident. Yamini Krishnamurthy[6] was here to dance the other day. The tickets were very low for such a star; the venue, the Exhibition Theatre, a ramshackle stage and auditorium walled with matting, floored with earth and the stage an uneven dais, carpeted, a couple of spotlights dangling on ropes and a faded red velvet curtain hanging unhappily on its ropes. Not your ideal theatre! But the audience was there. Real lovers of the art, the dancing daughters, the dowager mothers with diamonds in their noses and tissue saris scratching their neighbors, and the stragglers who have dropped in due to sheer tiredness of walking from the neighboring neon-clad gaudy brilliance of the shops in the Exhibition. Half the front foyer is thrown open to invitees, the select few friends of the conveners and their expanding families, the deputy secretaries and the I.A.S. officers and the people in official power. The ticket buyers are seated in the rear on uncomfortable chairs and worse floors. But then the dance is the thing? The performance is magnificent – the electric dancer and her vibrant singing sister and their heavily accented father. It does the heart good and the mind is elevated by the performance. Khajuraho never looked so good as in Yamini's Odissi numbers,[7] Andhra womanhood never so glorious as in her Kuchipudi, her wanton gestures, her easy flow from the classic *mudras* and *abhinaya* to a supple let-go of both body and hands and legs. And finally, Satyabhama so forlorn in her *virha*. An exquisite performance which, if in Bombay or Calcutta, would have brought rave notices from

---

6 Andhra-born Indian dancer Yamini Krishnamurthy, specialized in the Bharatanatyam and Kuchipudi classical genres.

7 Odissi, or Orissi, is a major Indian classical dance originated in the eastern state of Odisha.

the press – even if only in *Filmfare* or the Sunday *Statesman*. But in our town the papers did not even know that such an hour of glory was theirs the previous evening. One wakes up from such a show as from a dream, unreal, to the reality of the first cup of coffee.

And of course, its resistance to change! In the twenty years I have watched it grow, there does not seem to have been any face-lifting worth the expression. Of course, the streets are wider and the old buildings have made room for newer buildings and the traffic policemen have changed uniforms. But the basic pattern has not altered and the middle way continues its sway. The other day a new night club opened in town and, sitting in its dusky interiors, I realised that nothing was new, even here, and the faces of the people, the Punjabi floor-walker with his accent as thick as his belly, the Anglo-Indian manager with his clipped mustache and clipped accent, the familiar sights were as they were in similar night clubs many years ago. Saarinen's chairs were there, and wrought iron grilles and womb-like slit lamps, and the wooden floor and the red curtains on the windows, which stay shut permanently on account of air conditioning. Oh yes! To this extent it has changed. But the rest of the mood has not moved. There is a jukebox right in the middle of the floor with the latest Tony Brants and Mohd Hafis in equal proportions and there is the usual clientele. At one table the businessman is entertaining the government servant. And at another, a bunch of belles in ponytails and pedal pushers exchanging banter with the college cricket heroes. And here are the servers with their fierce moustaches on their green faces and light young eyes. There is a lot of beer being drunk and tandoori chicken being consumed. Keeping time with the times. But how dull the conversation, how unintelligent the general level of culture, and generally how poor the excitement. This is a town where everything happens elsewhere. Even when a major calamity had to happen it was a hundred miles away. The river never floods nor does the earth quake. The students strike at Sri Venkateswara University and the Taj is in Agra. The middle way is the best here for everything is in its ordered place, a mediocre brilliance of 'nothing happens in this of all possible places'.

But then, as I started out to imply, after all life is for the most part ordinary. The streets are full of ordinary people going out to their ordinary jobs on their second-hand scooters trying to satisfy their ordinary wives with extraordinary gifts, or send their children to the Convent School to hear them talk in English accents. On Charles Street the Indian Christians put up their many Christmas trees once a year and make believe that it is snowing outside and Santa Claus is on his way on a sleigh drawn by reindeers. And the schoolboys coming out of the picture house after a date with 'Bridgette Bardot' [sic] wistfully walk past the Percy's Hotel where an anemic hand is beating out a Beguine that Benny Goodman never began. And the fair Anglo-Indian girls in their faded cotton skirts, are competing with the dusky Indian women who shuffle past in their crisp raw silk saris as if they were born into that sort of thing. And the nouveau riche gather on Sunday mornings beneath the coloured umbrellas of the Sailing Club and watch the boats sail by while their life flows away with the beer that is being drained in from their pewter tankards. Such life is the norm in the city if one has money to spend and time to fritter. But then what is the norm of life but what is set by the people of the city. An ordinary people for the most part, with desires that are never fulfilled, cities never visited and fun never had. Eternally here and always away in the wonder land of fantasy. So it goes, so it goes. The *perpetuum mobile*! Till one day you are carried away down the street which you walked so many times before and a few friends brood over your loss and bereft relatives are shattered and the flowers in the graveyard smile wistfully at what has gone under.

And life continues to be in the city for others. A city on the map, in the ground, from the air, eternally with you because you are of it and the city is a part of you.

During 1944–47, I was a student of Engineering at Benares Hindu University when Dr S. Radhakrishnan was Vice-Chancellor,[8] but Benares was a dirty, crowded city and did not hold any attraction to an 18-year-old from the cantonment town of Secunderabad in the Nizam's state, thirsting for adventure. I never knew in those days that Benares was the home of Ravi Shankar, and the famous ghats were just ugly stone steps going down to a polluted river where half-burnt corpses were let out into the water. Many years later, when I saw *Pather Panchali*, I could not visualise it as the same city which Satyajit Ray's genius and camera had transformed into unforgettable settings for his film. The only place that I liked in the city was the Theosophical Society, which we would visit on Sunday evenings to hear a willowy young lass sing Meera *bhajan*s.

At Assi Ghat, near the University, I had also come across two Europeans, Raymond Burnier, a Swiss photographer, and Alain Daniélou, a French scholar, who lived in an old palace by the Ganges and sometimes visited the coffee house which was our daily haunt. I do not remember exactly how I came to meet them, but having met them, I soon fell prey to their accented English and their exotic way of life, their talk of Paris and London and New York, which they visited regularly. Raymond Burnier was the photographer of Konark and Khajuraho, which Stella Kramrisch, the noted Indologist, has made famous in her book *The Hindu Temple*; Alain Daniélou seemed to be doing research on antique Indian musical

---

8 Indian philosopher and academic Sarvepalli Radhakrishnan (1888–1975) served as Vice-Chancellor of Banaras Hindu University from 1939 until 1948, then as Vice President (1952–62) and President (1962–67) of India.

instruments, and later he became famous as a translator of the *Kamasutra*. The more they talked about the greatness of Indian culture, and the more I wanted them to talk of the Western world. Through them I discovered Picasso and Paul Klee, Beethoven and Mozart. Their home was a derelict palace on the river, with its slender stone balconies projecting onto the water, out of which they said that during the rainy season they could float their rubber boat into the river.

The curtains and drapes on the stone arches were old Benares saris of gaudy designs. 'We throw the women into the river and use their saris as curtains', Raymond used to jokingly remark, and my young and gullible mind almost believed it. Burnier's life-size photographs of the erotica of Khajuraho and Konark lay scattered all around the open courtyard, along with prints of Picasso and Salvador Dalí. And their occasional references to the celebrities of the art world of New York and Paris were simply too much for a wide-eyed innocent like me. There was an element of mystery hanging around their lives that eluded and enchanted me. I often wondered what they found in me, an awkward youth with bright eyes who talked his head off about everything around him.

However, it was at their house that I met Louis MacNeice, the British poet who was visiting India on a BBC assignment. It was the first of October 1947, according to my diary. Raymond had asked me to come to their place to meet a friend; I was late for the appointment, and Raymond chided me for my Indian punctuality. As usual I tried to laugh it off and Raymond calmly introduced the guest, 'meet Mr. Louis MacNeice from London…'.

The ground opened beneath me. I was speechless and silence froze into my mouth as I struggled to find some words. Louis MacNeice, Auden's fellow poet, the author of *Plant and Phantom* and *Letters from Iceland*, the very same poet whose 'Prayer before Birth':

I am not yet born; O hear me.
Let not the bloodsucking bat or the rat or the stoat or the
club-footed ghoul come near me.

I am not yet born, console me.
I fear that the human race may with tall walls wall me,

was as famous and familiar to me as Auden's 'Lay your sleeping head, my love / Human on my faithless arm.'

I had only recently read his autobiographical *Modern Poetry*, where he described his friends Auden, Isherwood, Spender et al.

He was seated behind a pillar, on the floor, hidden in the shadows of the twilight creeping into the room. In utter silence I watched his thick, long fingers delicately holding a cigarette, his loose body reclining uncomfortably on the soft carpets on the floor. Next morning Raymond invited me to join them on a drive around the city with MacNeice. Snuggled between the two great men, two foreign bodies, as the jeep drove back to the university through the dirty streets, under the dirty eyes of people staring, I asked endless questions to my first poet in the flesh.

'Is it true what you wrote about Lawrence, and were you still a virgin?'

And MacNeice straightened me out about whatever misconceptions I had about him.

'Lawrence was a beautiful stylist, a mood creationist, but somewhat tasselled… full of mannerisms… Sex was mere wishful thinking on his part... which he couldn't get rid of… his poems were better… Rhythmical repetitions…'

And from Lawrence to Rimbaud and Enid Starkie's biography, which I had just gotten hold of, and thence to Dalí's *Secret Life*…

'I don't much care for Dalí's philosophy… a great

draughtsman with a head full of ideas taken from books.'

Not once did MacNeice say anything except in reply to my questions. Typically British, I thought, not being too aware of the difference between the British and the Irish. He was dressed in khaki shorts and a bunyan (or T-shirt, as they are called now); a tall, angular face and deep blue eyes... irregular cigarette-stained teeth and yellowed fingers... an inveterate chain-smoker and a hesitant talker, charmingly sophisticated – but never, oh never poetic.

'Peshawar was a city I liked... mountains all round. New York is fantastic... wonderful to visit... unbearable to live in...' And when I quoted Auden ('Let us honour if we can / The vertical man / Though we value none / But the horizontal one'), he wondered if I had understood the religious overtones. 'Auden wrote readable poetry, quite lucid at times but lately too academic. Auden is a terrible reader of his poems... doesn't go out to meet people. Books, books, books, they stifle him. Day Lewis started out as a poor imitation of Auden but developed... very urbane, painstaking. Spender is muddle-headed, good only when he talks of something definite... a better critic than a poet. Oh yes, very effective looks, impressive, a bit of a show-off... The Isherwood of Mr Norris was perfect... a charming person but drawn away by Huxley and Swami Prabhavananda. Huxley the brilliant – talks prose, not talk. With beautifully chosen words he dominates the show like a precocious child at an adult party. Forster writes beautifully and strikes home better...'

Random thoughts and opinions literally spurted out of MacNeice, as I talked my head off with my newly acquired knowledge from books about these writers and their work.

Here am I, here are you
What does it mean, my dear
What does it mean?

Many years later, in his *Collected Poems*, I found two poems written in India, 'Letter from India' (addressed to his wife Heidi) and 'Mahabalipuram'. In the first he declares:

> And both of us are both, in either
> An India sleeps below our West,
> So you for me are proud and finite
> As Europe is, yet on your breast
> I could find too that undistressed
> East which is east and west and neither?

And on Mahabalipuram:

> But the visitor must move on and the waves assault the temple,
> Living granite against dead water, and time with its weathering
> action
> Make phrase and feature blurred;
> (....)
> Our ageing limbs respond to those ageless limbs in the rock
> Reliefs. Relief is the word.

Many years later, I remembered Auden and Isherwood and MacNeice and Spender and Isherwood in a poem called 'Gone Now':

> They are all gone
> Gone is the googly bowler
> And the cutter of stones
> And the maker of words
> Each has gone
> And left a void
> In my world of wood[9]

---

9 'Gone Now', *Selected Poems* (Calcutta: Writers Workshop, 1995): 82.

TO STANFORD

In 1947 the Nizam's State Government advertised study abroad scholarships in engineering, medicine, agriculture and other professional subjects of study. I, with my BA degree in mathematics and ten years of engineering at BHU (Banaras Hindu University),[10] applied for one of the scholarships in engineering and, as luck would have it, was selected. In my application I had chosen a specialisation in structures; however, all available openings were filled by applicants who had already qualified in civil engineering, and the committee offered me a scholarship in mechanical engineering with a specialisation in steel structures. At that time, if they had offered me a scholarship in horticulture I would have accepted it. This was the first silver lining in an otherwise bleak year, and I promptly applied to various universities in the United States. There was no doubt in my mind that I would go to the US, so Murthy[11] and I would spend all our free hours at the USIS library, reading about the golden land and dreaming of the opportunity that was beckoning us. Laboriously we filled out application forms, made true copies of our qualifications

---

10 Ten years at BHU is obviously a mistake, since in his 1972 piece 'A Bit of Me' Rayaprol says that he went 'to the University at Benares to study engineering' at around the time he was eighteen or nineteen. S. Rayaprol, 'A Bit of Me', *The Miscellany* (Calcutta) 49 (February 1972): 23–31.

11 Murthy V. N. Sripada (1927–1956) studied engineering at the University of California, Berkeley while Rayaprol was at Stanford. There, eager to pursue a literary career, he started calling himself Christopher (after Christopher Isherwood). Rayaprol wrote often about 'Chris' in his poetry and also left a short, unpublished prose portrait ('My Friend Murthy'), not included in this collection.

and testimonials in long hand, and air-mailed them to various universities in the United States. The red and blue bordered replies we received were a sight for sore eyes, even though they contained brief rejection slips. I applied to MIT, CIT,[12] Columbia, Michigan, UC Berkeley, UCLA, USC (Los Angeles), and Stanford University. I had set my mind on going to California, which was the golden land par excellence. California meant Hollywood, of which I knew so much through the movies and the movie magazines. Thanks to the movies and the technicolour travelogues of James FitzPatrick, I was transported to the magic world of blue skies and golden sands on the magic carpet of my dreams.

I liked the florid faces and the nasal twangs of the Americans, and the easy familiarity with which they lived their lives. And here at last was my opportunity to go to the land of my dreams. After nearly a year of waiting in agony and suspense, afraid of losing my scholarship if I wasn't admitted to an American university, I finally received acceptance letters from two universities in California. Stanford accepted me for the winter quarter commencing in January 1948, and USC for their second semester. Stanford granted me provisional admission to their master's programme as a transfer student, and USC offered me admission into their BS programme with credits for work already done. Though USC meant LA, at Hollywood's doorstep, and Stanford University was new to me, I opted for Palo Alto, forty miles south of San Francisco.

And then began the agonizing process of fulfilling the formalities for my departure: trudging to the secretariat behind my father to meet the relevant bureaucrats, all of whom my father addressed with easy familiarity in his half-baked Urdu; applying for a passport and then a visa, which had to be issued from Madras; drawing foreign exchange,

12 The California Institute of Technology, known as Caltech.

etc.; and finally buying a ticket to the United States. I was booked by Thomas Cook on the P. & O. R.M.S. 'Strathmore', leaving Bombay on 12 December 1947 to reach New York via London. Since I had to be present for my registration at Stanford University on January 5, 1948, I was granted special permission by the government, through the offices of my dear father, to fly from London to New York and thence to San Francisco. The officer in charge of scholarships assured my father that someone would meet me in London, New York, etc., and there would be no problem for a callow youth in any of these places. And since I was going to London by ship, they scheduled a huge crate of books and papers to be delivered to the High Commission of India. The days passed in a daze, and I found myself pushed by fate toward my destination. At that time the Hyderabad State was in the thick of the Razakar movement and the impending police action which was to change the destiny of the state.[13]

For safety reasons, my mother and sisters were sent across the border to Bapatla, Andhra, while I remained in Secunderabad with my father and a friend until I finally boarded a train to Bombay with my friend Venkat, whom my father had asked to accompany me. At Bombay I was to stay with a Dr. Sarmananda, a friend of my father but quite

---

13 The rakazars were a private militia organized by Hyderabad Muslims to resist the integration of the princely state in the Dominion of India. As a result of their terrorizing practices against Hindu villagers, in September 1948 the Indian Army invaded Hyderabad and forced the Nizam (princely ruler) to surrender. Although the six-day Operation Polo occurred without significant loss of civilian lives, it was later estimated that between 30,000 and 40,000 people lost their lives in the communal violence that accompanied what was misleadingly referred to as a 'police action'.

unlike him, a gentleman of questionable morals who lived with a Gujarati lady and spent his days buying and selling securities on the phone, which was his occupation. Dr. Sarmananda was an affable old man and I was happy that he treated me like a friend and not a child and even offered me a drink. He also took me and Venkat to a posh restaurant where he taught me rudimentary table manners, using knife and fork, and also made me buy a dressing gown, a felt hat and woolen underwear to battle against the cold of the west. The two or three days I spent in Bombay went by pleasantly enough, and on the fateful day I found myself at the Harbour on Ballard Pier No 11, to board the R.M.S. 'Strathmore'. My dear friend Venkat was with me, and when he came up the gangway to wish me bon voyage I could feel the trepidation with which I was setting foot in the unknown. But my eyes were set on America and nothing else seemed to matter. I do not remember being homesick or sad at leaving my family and friends, not being aware of the sacrifices my father had made to make this trip come true for me. I was 22 and just raring to go out of the country and into the unknown, where I was going to make a success of my life like the young Tom Edison on the brink of his discovery.

During the Second World War the 'Strathmore', like most ships of its size, had been converted into a troop ship and though it was almost two years since the war was over, it had not yet got back its original status. The state room to which I had been assigned contained about 24 bunk beds in three tiers with common bathing and toilet facilities, far from luxurious and much worse than my hostel room at BHU. But the general euphoria which surrounded me at the time, and the anticipation of the promised land, made me ignore such temporary shortcomings. My companions were mostly British men returning home from the Pacific front and were crude and made vulgar talk, most of which I could not understand. But I liked their rough manners and at night I would sleep in a haze, enveloped by the smell of beer and their sweaty bodies, and the rowdy words which they would fling at each other flew around my head. After the three meals, which was the only regular feature of the day, I would spend my time in the library or on a deck, or in one of the many lounges. The walks on the deck in the cold winter breeze were refreshing. I must have cut a comical figure in my thick khaki army surplus overcoat which a friend had given me, with the ridiculous felt hat that I could barely keep in place in the strong winds. At other times I sat in the cozy cushioned sofas in one of the lounges, with a book by Huxley or Maugham to keep me company. (Maugham's *Moon and Sixpence* and *Razor's Edge* were my frequent companions in those days.) I moved near the strains of a piano played by an Indian girl in her teens, accompanied by an old English governess. I imagined she was the daughter of some rich Indian businessman going to her finishing school in Europe. The sight of her frail figure seated on the stool, striking chords on the piano and sending waves of nostalgia across the room, was my first experience of romantic unrequited love. I would follow her to the dining room and watch her from a not too far, not too near table in silence. This one-way romance lasted all of the thirteen days of my voyage through Aden and Port Said and Gibraltar, till we entered the Bay of Biscay. From there it was a stormy crossing till we disembarked at Tilbury Docks on the 27 December 1947, under overcast skies in a gray, cold, typically British weather.

It was an overnight flight from Washington, DC, and when I landed in San Francisco it was a chilly, grey morning with a heavy fog and light rain. As the plane descended on the Bay, I sat in my seat dozing, my mind full of feelings of the new world into which, it seemed, I had been suddenly catapulted. Fifteen days on the R.M.S. 'Strathmore' and four days in London hadn't done it, but twenty four hours from London, when the plane stopped at Gander[14] and was delayed for half a dozen hours due to bad weather, I felt as if I was really getting into a new world at last. A world full of snow, as it appeared in Gander, with Canadians who were 6 feet tall and 2 feet wide, with ruddy faces; and then New York with more snow, the automobiles abandoned in the street as a result of the incredible storm.[15] But it was a world such as I had not quite dreamed of, in spite of Hollywood movies and the Reader's Digest and *Look* magazine. I realised that America was all that and more, too. The speed of living was quite unlike anything I was used to, the friendly smiling faces of the people, too, were a surprise to me, coming from a land where life always seemed too serious to smile or laugh about. I was coming to this new world with the hope and ambition and the desire to cast away all the past and especially my failure at Benares, and find a new dawn. I did not quite know what to expect, for reality always turned out somewhat different from what one had read about or expected. I was young, with a sharp mind and a fervent imagination, and if I was self-conscious, I did not feel so. How else could I explain having two breakfasts at Gander airport, one at 2 am and another at eight? And did I not indulge in all the different cereals that I found at the breakfast table, plus Aunt Jemima's pancakes with maple syrup, plus bacon and eggs of two kinds, which made me enjoy the country and its people and get into their spirit?

All these thoughts were with me on that plane ride to San Francisco, and when I got off the plane that chilly January morning, I must have been quite a sight in my army trench coat, borrowed from a friend who was employed in an ordnance

---

14 Gander International Airport in Newfoundland, Canada.

15 The Great Blizzard of 1947, which hit the northeastern United States on Christmas Day and lasted almost twenty-four hours, leaving New York City paralized under a thick blanket of snow.

depot, and my English-style, tight at the waist, form-fitting tweed suit and Italian hat. Perhaps I looked lonely and forlorn, for I remember someone asking me where I wanted to go. I said Palo Alto and asked where I could catch a train or a bus to get there. I was given elaborate directions to either catch a train from the railway station, or to get on a Greyhound at the bus terminal, and neither prospect appealed to me. And right then and there, a yellow cab driver approached me and said he'd take me to Palo Alto along with some other people for 5 dollars. We would get there in little over an hour. It seemed cheap and quick, so I got into the cab and sat wedged between the door and a young couple who snuggled and made love to each other for the entire ride, as if I did not exist.

THE PHYSICS OF COLOUR
the Art of Jamini Roy

So little is known of Jamini Roy's life, either as a published fact or a heard truth, that I would like to say at the very outset that the meagre biographical details which I will refer to are culled from several random sources and will, I hope, serve the reader merely to form a broad idea of the background of the artist's life in relation to his work. And then again, so much of his work is in evidence these days, not only his own prolific works which are easy and inexpensive to acquire, but also works very much influenced by him, and which serve eminently as drawing room décor in upper middle-class homes in India. One cannot help coming across words like colour, folk art, etc., when one talks about the work of Jamini Roy. While it is true that he has *discovered* colour for our eyes, the way one sees colour in India, the reds and browns of the earth, the black of human bodies, and while it is true that a superficial appraisal of his pictures would at once bring to mind the naïve images of rural Indian life, such an analysis is an oversimplification of the issue that reduces the real worth of the painter, and also a more complete enjoyment of his work. It is true that broken walls of barns in Indian villages might have carried wonderfully alive pictures; it is true that in inaccessible parts of India, craftsmen bound by tradition and prejudice practice their lonely trades and produce masterpieces in wood, pottery etc. But as a point of fact, the average Indian has not seen them, or if his eyes happen to have passed over such things, he has really not discovered their beauty isolating them from the dross and filth which usually surrounds them. Till it was left for Jamini Roy to come along and rediscover it all for us; and in his single-minded search for beauty and colour he has brought it to us on canvas, to be hung in a frame, on a wall.

I am thinking of that famous picture of Jamini Roy which I have carried with me halfway round the world, hanging on a wall or sitting on a shelf, ready to leap out of its frame like the proverbial Bengal tiger:

> On my wall in my room
> is a blue woman whom
> I have fixed in the midst
> of a dance
>
> Fish for eyes and her hands
> painted red (for in my country
> they like the colour) her feet
> big and weighted by metal rings
>
> Her lips lowered in all modesty
> a white ring in the only showing
> ear, a yellow dress which is all about.
> Naked yet, and shy.[16]

The movement of the dance is implicit rather than explicit, as each colour *dances off* each other to suggest rhythmic movement:

> Blue is the colour
> Not only in the sky's naked behind
> Not only in the sea's upward heave
> Blue is the colour
> Blue-eyed, blue-haired, blue woman
> Not only in you
>
> Indigo-scented afternoon hiding

---

16 'The Blue Woman' (see p. 41).

Between the thighs of the night
Blue woman on the wall with the white fish eyes
Blue is the colour of your movement
Settled into a yellow quiet.[17]

Long after the picture has been forgotten, the effect of its blues and yellows remains on the mind of the viewer. And not only yellow and blue, but brown as of earth or a naked arm, and black as of a man's throat, a man who is an Indian, a Santhal from the forest.

I am thinking of the 'Head of the Santhal' and 'Santhal Mother and Child', the masculinity of the one and the utter delicacy of the other. Both executed in the same basic colours and every visible detail, or that little there is of it, similar. And yet, it is the column of the neck of this man, strong as the forest that must have given him birth, and the little red circles in the other that remind us, ever so subtly, of the village home from which mother and child have come.

I am thinking of his 'Red Horse' with its reds and yellows and browns and the little touch of life he has given what is, in every other respect, a wooden toy horse, by painting not a flying mane or tail, as one would expect, but a green eyeball as round, terribly awake and flaring as any carousel horse. I can think of no other artist whose colours alone seem to convey meanings subtly and all by themselves, quite independent of the forms they fill.

Yellow and Blue
is a way of flight
the apple is true
and her arm a night
long sadness. Her eye

---

17 Unpublished.

a white fish of form
and her lip a lie
that the worm
forgot to chew;
for the apple became
an egg and the two
eyes being the same.

Yellow and blue
is a colourless silence.
The bird is new
and the brown fence
does not surround
her fish-white eye
A green round thigh
breaks on the yellow
of the egg,
the earth being slow
in turning to dust.[18]

But then of course he has always been an artist dedicated to his work, unsure perhaps where he was leading to, but definitely in pursuit of a vague dream, shall we say, of lost childhood, of memories of village life which he must have experienced as a child, of dolls and clay pots with coloured gods on them. As an artist his development has been gradual but sure. It is obvious that he has learnt to walk before attempting to run, for he has perfected every necessary artifice of his art. Colour, line, tone, form – he is a master of every little detail. Nothing haphazard in his work. The magnificent sweep of his lines, especially when drawing a woman's shape; the brevity of his brush strokes are no accidents, and the balance of colours and

---

18 'Yellow and Blue' (see p. 40–41).

shapes! One might imagine that he must have had quite a classical training, if not exactly copying models – he had gone through portraiture and landscapes and it is known that for several years he lived as a successful portrait painter. But even so, his portraits tended to be more Whistlerian than Royal Academic. It is also obvious that he has studied deeply the work of other painters, including contemporaries like Picasso and Klee. Going through a gallery of his pictures one is tempted to believe that, like the work of every great artist, his shows the assimilated effects of every great artist before him. Not the effects of imitation, if that's the right word, but of the principles that have made these predecessors original, and which now make his own work original and unique, so that in the final analysis, they are his own. His search for configurations of form and colour, his achievement of a simplicity of line, and his learning to shed inessentials, have in Roy's case been no different from that of any other artist's search for truth and beauty. And in essence it is a struggle, a tortuous search for truth, the meaning of life itself, the discovery of humanity, and the final peace with oneself if not with the world. And in each artist's case this struggle is different only insofar as the geographic condition is different. Jamini Roy belonged to a half-English, middle-class society in India at a time when the difference between the class to which he belonged by birth, and the masses of people outside his doorstep, so to speak, was an important factor in his artistic growth and liberation. At a certain stage of his life, he had the courage to discard everything he knew and had learned as an artist, and to plunge in the dark: a certain light within his head must have been his only direction.

He is now almost seventy. He was born in a village in Bengal, the son of a small landowner. Growing up in the latter half of the nineteenth century, in a middle-class household in

Bengal could certainly not provide any striking background for his artistic development. He must have shared, but only superficially, like every other Indian, the heritage of the rural culture in which he was born and brought up. The work of the native artisans must have been hidden somewhere deep in his subconscious when he decided to become an artist, for his early training at Calcutta's Government College of Art was no more spectacular than anyone else's. Based on samples of his work from this period, it is obvious that he followed different schools at different times. Early landscapes, done in the best academic style, portraits at which he worked for nearly ten years, then a conventional rejection of all Western influences and a return to the methods of old Indian painting. Even so, it must have been frustrating for him to give up a successful career as a portrait painter to enter a period of artistic isolation and material poverty. But such loneliness, such an intense search for the fundamentals of art and its relationship to the life of people, must have had a lasting influence on his mind. And this must have sustained him through the long and lean years of poverty and hunger, of cold nights and the problem of keeping his family alive. It is said that he was living, at that time, in a corner of Calcutta where the sun could rarely enter. There he mixed his own paints and made his own canvasses, for he could not afford to buy them; painting on whatever surface he could get: paper, wood or gunny sack. And like a blind man at first seeing the light, he discovered the blacks of lamp-black, the reds of the geru stone, the yellows and ochre of coarse, handwoven cloth. There, fumbling in the dark, he developed his own personal expression, a style, a rhythm completely his own and which is an affirmation of the life that he found in his own people. Surely, during that period, his eyes must have gone deep and straight to his own childhood and the work of the village craftsmen, painters of dolls made of wood for the children of God, the makers of clay pots, the weavers of cloth, the makers of the stylised 'pats' with their brevity of line. There, surely, the colours in his brain, the sweeping curves and ascetic lines, the flat stylised bodies and the massive shapes of human flesh bound by delicate lines, must have evolved into the patterns and style for which he is known today.

But during all those years there was no recognition. It is said that it was only by accident that Mukul Dey, who had returned from Europe and was the Principal of the Government College of Art at Calcutta, discovered his old friend Jamini Roy and the masterpieces that he was creating. And it was largely through his efforts that Roy's art came to be recognized. Success came slowly but surely, so that today Jamini Roy occupies a position as one of the greatest living artists of India. In the particular style which he has so successfully developed, he produces nearly a dozen pictures a day. He paints mostly on tempera and his pictures are not very expensive, as a remembrance of his own lean days. Today he draws much critical attention, and it is easy for critics to categorize his work as folk art or regional art, thus undervaluing his real greatness.

But today Jamini Roy has found his peace with himself and his art. Does he paint the blood of his people? Is there anything more than pure pictorial appeal in his painting? What is his take on today's world? Confronted with such questions, he has really nothing to say. Discover, if you can, your own truths in regard to his work. Look deep and you will discover his great love for humanity, his humour, his sincere joy at the sight of God's wonderful creations. Would you want anything more by way of comment? Just look around with your eyes open this time, and you'll see what he has done to your eyes. Are you Indian? Do you know villages in Bengal? ... But it really doesn't matter.

HEART CONDITION

I had always known that something was amiss with my heart but I'd never thought that this Old Faithful would ever betray me. But this afternoon, way out there in the treeless wilderness, the tigers were really burning bright. You know how it is when you are OK. Your heart is a joke and your liver an excuse to drink a little less than what you wish.

And yet, hours later, I am unable to describe my symptoms clearly to the doctor. A giddiness? Yes, but rather as if the brain were swimming in a turbulent ocean of blood. Weakness? Yes. Yes, but rather as if my legs were floating on air. Pain in the region of the heart? But undefinable, dull and acute at once. And really it is hard to say if the pain is physical or mental. The romantic heart and the anatomic heart have gotten into a conspiracy to fool you.

Why then the anxiety? To get home at all costs. To see the ones you love, to sleep on your own bed and watch the tracery of leaves through the window. Beyond the trees it could be the sea or the mountains. But it is only your street with familiar houses and children shouting and cars turning the corner.

What you want, then, is things in their place. Love in the heart and order in the mind. Tomorrow after today. But only a few hours back, driving in the jeep, you wondered if you were ever going to live out the hour, and all the unfinished threads of your life broke in a tangle over your bewildered brain. So, a revaluation becomes necessary. You are getting to be forty. Successful to a degree, moderate, but just above the average. But all the dreams will remain dreams with you. (I thought this was the time to stop if it didn't seem too dramatic – indeed!).

So it goes. Your urine is clear and the feces without traces of impurities. The blood is as red as it ought to be. The human engine never seems to fail as it serves one master at a time.

Going for donkey's years, they say. Keep going, dear heart, march onward Christian soldiers, in the cause of the free.

And so to revaluations. Your family. Is their need the only reason? Or your friends. Whose need? Yours? One keeps going in spite of these questions. And for the moment the doctor is your dearest friend, as he stands between you and the door. The great rescuer. He with the pins and pills. The true saviour, for while the others can only offer you their sympathy, he is the one who acts – is indeed in command of your body, and for the moment your soul. Suddenly you are afraid. You place everything in his hands. Your life, your WILL that would not unbend ever before for love or money, now bends to itself when this thing Death stares at you. Are you really going to die? Are you REALLY.... Suddenly it is all down to a silly answer to a silly question. Your existence. This mountain of your LIFE.

And so to evaluations. You are sixty-six inches tall and nine stones heavy. Brown of skin and not too ugly. They said your eyes were good before they got red. And your nose is only slightly crooked. The ears are stiff and small but the head is large, and you have a mouth meant for kissing. You are intelligent... brilliant at school but a little less so in later years. You even flunked a year at college but for good reasons. And you were versatile. Like Leonardo. As you wanted to believe. You wrote poems on graph sheets, instead of cycles and charges. The poems were bad. But it was a march over the others. None of the others could poetise for nuts. They pushed slide rules and were good with the chisels. But you were a poet. A half-poet and half-engineer. So you look for a name. The secret life of Srinivas Rayaprol. An engineer by day and a poet by night. A unique combination and almost unbeatable. You continue to write and begin to publish in magazines like NEUROTICA, SYMBOLICA, GRAFFITI. You look for the odd ones. Homosexuality is a good bet. Necropolis. That's a lovely word. Once you wrote a poem titled AUTOMATA, a raucologue of the DEAD: A twist with the words. A way with the unrhyme. Gauche as they come. You smell roses and liken them to armpits. Delicious lusts. Viola: a poet is in the embryonic womb. Life is beginning to take shape. Break thy moorings and dare in a new found land. No boats behind and in no hurry to look ahead. Sweet 25.

Meanwhile you catch up on your work. It isn't hard to write a poem a month and build a bridge in a year. You are in love with life and the world of wood is comfortably building its shell around you. Love thy wife and raise a family. And, just to be different, be bisexual. Get your kicks both ways. Man, that's living! Practice on the one makes perfect with the other. Sex is a lovely limbo in which you wallow full-bodied, and full-throated. And your mind is a beautiful microcosm outside this banality which can take in all this ugliness and report back with such grace. The perfect poet. You bloom as Dorian and wither as Gray.

You sleep soundly eight hours a night but wake up quite unrefreshed. You cannot lie down in the darkness of your bed, nor muster up strength for a walk in the sun.

And the evening descends subtly on the languoring soul – afternoon – weary and full of lassitude. And the colours change before your eyes. The afternoon reds and yellows giving way to shades of grey and blue, orange and pink sunsets tinged with gold, the green and brown trees standing in solid silhouette. The lonely wail of a mullah piercing through the pierced stone *jalis* of the mosque and spilling out on to the sunset still. And the usual city sounds of automobiles and shouts of children and the howling of an occasional dog. Dear dirty Secunderabad, how I love you.

And love always ends in the afternoon, and on the wasted bed, the wasting lovers having nothing but regret and uncertainty left.

'You do love me still?'

'Yes... Yes... Yes...'

'When do we see each other again?'

'Tomorrow.'

'Almost twelve hours away?'

'Perhaps you'll stop loving me by then.'

'And I may not look for you either.'

Perhaps! Doubts and fears of not being loved forever, in life as in death. But how does one love in death? Physical death is not beautiful. And love loves to love life. I'll kiss your dying lips in a poem, but the flesh has cracks and fissures, and, bereft of the power of life, is unable to kiss back, to hurt or be hurt. It is not easy to love Death. Love life and death will love you.

Still the ambiguous limbo continues. They say nothing is wrong with me but I do not feel quite as well as I ought to be. My pride is hurt that I, too, have been a victim, suckered into the sickroom, so to say. And I remember how I always felt life to be like. A dare to do things. To drink more, do more, be more. And always there. And now they say I mustn't climb stairs, ride jeeps, do not do anything that isn't unnecessary. Take it easy. For what? Is it so necessary, this life that I have yet to live?

The weakness in the legs continues, and the heart sends out signals of pain. And the brain throbs and aches to keep up with this body. Oh, but that this mind could be put to rest.

Can thou not minister to a mind so diseased? And questions and answers, doubts and disbeliefs. If I die? If it dies? If the world comes to an end for me? For my loved ones? For my dependents? Always these shackles. Worn one after the other. Love and marriage and children and responsibilities for which your body is the respondent. Selling the car or buying jewelry, taking the kids to an exhibition. Normal acts of living that become duties and responsibilities to which you are bound.

I sit on the toilet and shout to the encroaching walls, 'My God, my God, why hast thou forsaken me?'

How does one define greatness? That it was a 66-year-old man, frail of body, sparkling eyes and squeaky voice, a paediatrician by day and a poet by night, a man full of wisdom and wit, overflowing with warmth of humanity and yet a no-nonsense person who had made it equally well in the world of men as in the world of letters. A poet of the stature of Eliot and Pound, who chose to live an uneventful existence not more than half a mile from where he was born. In the Oscar Williams anthology of modern verse, William Carlos Williams has only one page to eleven of Pound and twenty of Wallace Stevens,[19] both his contemporaries, although over a span of fifty years he published nearly forty volumes of original poetry, which is a larger output than Eliot's or Stevens'. Not that he wasn't well known as a poet, for he won practically every prize awarded for poetry in the US, including the National Book Award, the Dial Award, the Bollingen Prize, the Pulitzer Prize for Poetry and the Gold Medal for Poetry of the National Institute of Arts and Letters in May 1963, a few months after his death. It was just that he hated to talk of himself. 'Nine-tenths of our lives is well forgotten in the living,' he says in the foreword to his autobiography. 'Of the part that is remembered, the most had better not be told.' But the list of his friends reads like a dazzling roll of the artists and writers who have contributed significantly to the world of art and literature in the twentieth century – Ezra Pound, T. S. Eliot, Wallace Stevens, e.e. cummings, Hart Crane, Charles Demuth, Marsden Hartley,

---

19 In *The Pocket Book of Modern Verse: English and American Poetry of the Last Hundred Years from Walt Whitman to Dylan Thomas*, ed. Oscar Williams (New York: Pocket Books, 1954), Williams is represented by one poem ('The Yachts'), Pound by seven, and Stevens by fifteen.

Marianne Moore, H.D., James Joyce, Gertrude Stein, Marcel Duchamp, Brancusi, Juan Gris, Sylvia Beach, Margaret Anderson, Jane Heap, Nancy Cunard and many others. The list is unending. Those were the years of the *Little Review* and *transition*, *Dial*, and *Poetry*, of the Lost Generation and Surrealism, Dadaism and Imagism, and though at various times Williams was associated with all these movements, and the various art forms which they generated, he was always a 'loner' in the world of letters, always uniquely himself.

Williams was born on September 17, 1883, of an English father and a Puerto Rican mother at Rutherford, New Jersey, a small town of about 15,000 people, less than an hour's drive from New York City. And in this suburban village he lived most of his life, until he died on March 4, 1963. He was schooled in Rutherford's public schools and later at the Horace Mann High School in New York. In between he spent a year and a half in schools in Switzerland and Paris. From Horace Mann, Williams went straight to the medical school at the University of Pennsylvania, where he graduated with an M.D. in 1906. After a brief internship in hospitals in New York City and a stint at Leipzig, where he specialised in paediatrics, he returned to Rutherford in 1910, set up practice, married his girlfriend of three years, and bought the house at 9 Ridge Road where he settled down for the rest of his life. While at the University of Pennsylvania he met Ezra Pound, Hilda Doolittle, who was a classmate of Marianne Moore at Bryn Mawr, and Charles Demuth, the painter, who was studying at the Drexel Institute and eating at the same boarding house. Besides the influence that these friends had on the development of his literary career, Williams was reading Keats and Villon (in French), and Rabelais and Whitman. Ezra Pound was, of course, way ahead and always chiding Williams for his lack of education and reading. Even so, Williams kept his thoughts and notebooks to himself and the only time he took them for advice to an English professor, one Arlo Bates, at the insistence of his brother Ed, who was then studying architecture at MIT, the results were disastrous. The professor was very kind and complimented the young poet on a creditable imitation of Keats' line and form, and finally advised him to go on with his medical studies.

But the decision to write was made many years earlier and Williams was not to be deterred. Let me quote from his autobiography:

> The big fight came at the beginning, when I was making up my mind what to do with my incipient life. [...]
>
> The preliminary skirmish concerned itself with which art I was to practice. Music was out... Painting – fine, but messy, cumbersome. Sculpture?... To dance?... Words offered themselves and I jumped at them.... I wanted to write and writing required no paraphernalia. [...]
>
> That having been decided, forever, what to do about my present objective, medicine? Should I give it up? Why? First, no one was ever going to be in a position to tell me what to write... No one and I meant no one (for money) was ever (never) going to tell me how or what I was going to write. That was number one. Therefore, I wasn't going to make any money by writing. Therefore, I had to have a means to support myself while I was learning... I was going to work for it, with my hands, which I had been told (I know it anyhow) were stone-mason's hands. I also looked at my more or less stumpy fingers and smiled. An esthete, huh? Some esthete. [...]

And so the die was cast. He had decided to write and he had decided to make his living as a doctor. No conflict at all. And in fact it was his medicine which gained him entrance to the secret gardens of his self, the world within, that he wanted to tell openly. So he wrote of the bad boys and girls, the renegades and dirty-minded, deaths and births, the negro woman 'carrying a bunch of marigolds, wrapped in an old newspaper... the bulk of her thighs causing her to waddle as she walks...', a poor old woman 'munching a plum on the street a paper bag of them in her hand...', the young housewife (who) 'moves about in negligee behind the wooden walls of her husband's house', the crowd at the ball game 'moved uniformly by a spirit of uselessness which delights them...', and so on. But while some of his poems are full of what is coarse, ugly and commonplace, others are full of what is clear, delicate and beautiful and rare. For Williams also speaks of 'her body not so white as anemone petals nor so smooth – nor so remote a thing', of 'asphodel, that greeny flower, like a buttercup upon its branching stem', and of 'the Yachts that contend in a sea which the land partly encloses.' Williams was an Imagist poet, but not of the Stevens kind or the Marianne Moore variety. There is always, in his words, the familiar, the America that Randall Jarrell describes in despair as 'the America of poets.' At the time of writing this article, I have been reading Gore Vidal's *Kalki* and am suitably impressed by the cleverness of such writing. And I remember what Williams had to say. In one of his letters to me, commenting on the literary scene of the early 1950s in New York, he wrote, 'When I think of what style has come to mean, I want to puke. A clever English literary style, an Oxford accent in the writing, with proper disregard for everything commented upon, an indirected puffing of their own containments using the American background as a field to enhance the highlights of their own charm, is about as low as anyone can get as a writer.'

Those were the days when Eliot's *Cocktail Party* was a big hit on the New York stage, when the eastern college campuses were the ivory towers and breeding grounds for the poets turned professors of literature or the other way around, and Dylan Thomas was wowing then with his outrageous poetry readings from coast to coast. I am also an admirer of Dylan Thomas but from way back and so I wrote to Bill about the discovery of Dylan Thomas by literary America. His response was immediate, '... I have found it impossible to go to hear Dylan Thomas, while he was here. Just the dreamy look that comes into the eyes of our half-assed writers and so called competent critics – who control the publicity columns of the avant-garde forums and publications has been enough for me. They drool at the mouth. You can see that they are wetting in their pants out of excitement over his voice and the wild colors of his imagery... what they cannot see is that American poems are of an entirely different sort from Thomas's Welsh-English poems. They use a different language and operate under a different compulsion. They are more authoritarian, more Druidical, more Romantic – and they are, truly, more colorful. WE CAN'T AND MUST NOT WRITE THAT WAY...'

In a sense, it was this local pride that lay at the bottom of most of his writing. Williams was a great champion of the American heritage. In *In the American Grain*, one of his earliest works, he makes an attempt at re-definition, to supplant the new with the old. And his last great opus, *Paterson,* is basically about the re-establishment of old values and the men and women who gave America its unique character. *Paterson* consists of five parts and an unfinished sixth part, it was written over nearly 15 years from 1946 to 1960, and is about an industrial town fused with the entire life of a man, who is Williams himself. During the period of its writing, Williams suffered at least two strokes, one of which crippled his arm, leg, face and, partly, his speech, and forced him to punch the keys of his typewriter with one hand. It is a magnificent poem, a statement of the Universality of Man and the search for a redeeming language. It traces the early origins and colonial history of Paterson, the city, and is full of snatches of memories, letters, impressions of scenes and people, scandal, grandiose and confusing sex, and makes symbolic use of the river Passaic running its course to the sea. A work at once grand and confusing. 'Words are the burden of poems, poems are made of words,' Williams has said, and in *Paterson* he has used both free words and controlled verse, but basically his poetic line has been organically welded to American speech like muscle to bone. In *Paterson* he has, in a sense, fulfilled his ambition to adopt any form or no form at all with perfect indifference, writing regular lines which scan perfectly or not, as the occasion demanded.

'Only my writing (when I write) is myself; only that is the real me in any essential way. Not because I bring to literature and to life two different inconsistent sets of values. No, I don't do that; and I feel that when anyone does it, literature is turned into just so much intellectual excrement fit for the same stinking hole as any other kind.'

My own acquaintance with 'Bill' Williams goes back to the early Fifties when I was a student of civil engineering at Stanford University and trying to make out as a poet. Was that a contradiction? Not really, for I was a graduate in literature as well as in engineering in India before going to Stanford, and I had had a fairly good grounding in English literature, and as a student of engineering at Benares Hindu University I had spent more of my time with Eliot and Auden and Isherwood than on the drawing board. And here now in the first flush of my freedom on the lovely Stanford campus and intoxicated with the California sun and the wines of Salinas County, I had my bellyful of literature, discovering for the first time Hart Crane and Henry Miller, Tennessee Williams and Truman Capote. Berkeley was only 40 miles away and Dizzy Gillespie was beating out bebop in San Francisco. And to a young Brahmin boy from Hyderabad, Andhra Pradesh, of 23, it was overwhelming and exhilarating and all too much. Of course I had to write poetry. Of course I had to have problems with Timoshenko's Theory of Elasticity, what with the whole day spent in school and half the night spent reading and writing 'literature.' Prof. Yvor Winters was then teaching poetry at Stanford and one semester I registered for one of his poetry-writing courses. But like Prof. Arlo Bates, he too was not kind to my efforts in poetry. He felt that I did not have the proper background, and suggested I start by reading his work *In Defense of Reason*, which was all about Modern American Poetry. I was piqued by Prof. Winters's criticism and not terribly taken by his book either. Except for one fact: that it gave me an introduction to a startlingly new poet, one William Carlos Williams, whom Prof. Winters often quoted in his book, to show the pitfalls of, and his own disdain for, free verse as opposed to traditional verse. Whatever that may have been, I caught on to the charm and depth of William Carlos Williams, whose *Selected Poems* had just been released by New Directions. Further research on this newfound love of mine revealed that the poet William Carlos Williams was also a successful physician living at 9 Ridge Road, Rutherford, New Jersey. So, I promptly took my problem there. And pat came the reply from the great man himself:

> It's a pleasure to have you come to me with your problem! Not that it isn't a problem with us all to know what to do with our lives, but in the case of a young poet it is more the normal than anything else situated as you are. The solution is without solution except writing. If you write well, you have the solution in your hands. If you write poorly that's an end to it. Every man must live as he may.
>
> Winters is an old acquaintance, by letter. We don't need to discuss either his critical position or his methods of attack. I disagree with him top and bottom as heartily as you seem to. His very intelligence

> seems to unseat him. It is not at all necessary for you to follow him.[20]

So I had found a friend. We exchanged more letters and when in the winter of 1950 I found myself in New York on vacation, I wrote to Dr. Williams that I would like to meet him. He wrote back immediately, and though he had misspelt my name, his welcome was warm and genuine. He gave me precise directions:

> The bus will be marked Paterson, Passaic, Rutherford. Get off at the Rutherford R.R. station and walk up the main business street 2 short blocks. Our house is the first one you come to with grass and a big tree in front of it on the left hand side just off the business section where Ridge Road begins. You can't miss it, it is the first house on Ridge Road.[21]

And so, on a cold Sunday afternoon in January, at around 5 PM, I found myself at 9 Ridge Road. It was a memorable meeting to say the least. I rang the bell and almost immediately the door was opened by a handsome white-haired lady whom I knew was Bill's wife Floss. Small of build but with a strong German face. And behind her was Bill. An old man with balding head and steel-rimmed glasses. He was dressed in corduroy pants and a checked shirt open at the neck and a brown tweed jacket. They took me into a large drawing room with a whole wall lined with shelves to the ceiling and bursting with books.

---

20 Letter from Williams to Rayaprol, 24 October 1949. Reproduced in *Why Should I Write a Poem Now: The Letters of Srinivas Rayaprol and William Carlos Williams, 1949–1958*, ed. G. Krätli (Albuquerque, NM: The University of New Mexico Press, 2018), 32.

21 Letter from Williams to Rayaprol, 6 January 1950. *Why Should I Write a Poem* Now, 33.

We sat in old, comfortable chairs, opposite a log fire to which Bill occasionally added a log or two. There I was, with two years of Stanford behind me and all the wealth of experience that a first-class university had to offer, and on the top of the world. My background of Auden and Isherwood was ideal to my discovery of Wallace Stevens and Hart Crane. And here was my latest discovery, the poet William Carlos Williams in the flesh no less. I must have talked my head off and Bill was a good, if amused listener. Floss served us tea and cookies. I could see her moving in the background, whistling some tune or other and adding a word or two to our conversation. I do not remember much of what Bill said, but he filled me in with details of the literary life in New York. He told me to see the Brancusi exhibition at the Museum of Modern Art and catch a Casals concert if I could. He gave me the addresses of cummings and Stuart Davis and a few others in Greenwich Village, but warned me not to get too involved with that sort of people. He showed me a monograph which he was writing for a Picasso exhibition to be held soon at the Louis Carre Gallery on 5th Avenue. But he never talked of his work except by way of answers to my many questions. He showed me his dispensary and the rickety typewriter on which he dashed off his daily dozen, as he called them, and his old car on which he made his rounds. Evening shadows were now falling and Floss came by and asked me to stay on for dinner. 'Nothing special, mind you,' she said, 'Bill will be with us, that's our son, and we'd like you to meet him.' Bill Jr. was also a doctor and later took over his father's practice. It was truly a simple dinner. We had some sherry to go with the roast pork and vegetables and black coffee later in the drawing room. Bill Jr. was genuinely curious about India, as many young men of that age were then (he was around 38 or 39), and I must have disappointed him with my ignorance of my country's politics. India had just become a republic, Gandhi was gone and Nehru had become the man of the hour. Anyway, we talked and talked. Around 9, Bill Jr. said he'd have to go. 'He lives quite close here with his wife and kids,' Floss explained, but made no attempt to ask him to stay which seemed odd to me at that time, steeped as I was in the Indian family tradition where a son cannot stay away from his parents even if he is married.

I, of course, made no attempt to move. There was so much to discuss. About poetry and music and the arts, about New York and Paris. Bill told a few anecdotes about Ezra Pound and his antics, about his own rejection slips, about some of his patients, about his friend and philosopher, Charles Sheeler, whose photograph of Williams was on the mantlepiece and which I coveted, along with a copy of *Kora in Hell* which I found on the bookshelf. Williams reluctantly gave me the book with a promise that I return it as soon as I had done with it, but did not part with the picture which was inscribed by Sheeler himself. (He later sent me an identical copy to India.)

About an hour later, Floss came round again and suggested that I stay over for the night – the last bus having left by then – and she'd make a bed for me in Bill Jr's room in the attic. Which she did, God bless her, and provided me with an extra blanket, as it was getting to be quite chilly and there was no heat in the attic.

I do not know whether I have been able to convey the warmth and utter humanness of Bill Williams in the above account of our meeting, but that was how he was. A great poet but a greater human being. A total person without sham or pretence, or a shred of artificiality in his being. I met him once more, a year later in New York, when we toured the museums and had lunch at one of the Italian places on 52nd Street. But these two brief meetings were enough to establish for me one of my most meaningful relationships. And over the years we wrote quite often to each other. He almost always replied. With his own fingers on that rickety typewriter and with his name Bill scrawled at the end, the writing getting more and more ungainly after his paralytic strokes. Only once Floss replied, because Bill had had another stroke and it would be some time before he could get well enough to write himself.

In the 80 years that he lived, William Carlos Williams produced several volumes of verse, short stories, essays, plays and articles and thousands of letters. It is amazing how he found time to do all this in spite of his full-time occupation as a paediatrician. Somewhere in his autobiography, he has described this:

> Five minutes, ten minutes, can always be found. I had my typewriter in my desk. All I needed was to pull up the leaf to which it was fastened and I was ready to go. I worked at top speed. If a patient came in at the door while I was in the middle of a sentence, bang would go the machine – I was a physician. When the patient left, up would come the machine. My head developed a technique; something growing inside me demanded reaping. It has to be attended to. Finally after eleven at night, when the last patient had been put to bed, I could always find the time to bang out ten or twelve pages. In fact, I couldn't rest until I had freed my mind from the obsessions which had been tormenting me all day. Cleansed of that torment, having scribbled, I could rest.

For a better understanding of the man, one has only to read *The Selected Letters of William Carlos Williams*, edited by John C. Thirlwall. These letters addressed during the period from 1902, when he was a medical student, to 1950 when he was living in retirement at Rutherford, bring out his personality even better than his autobiography, which he was reluctant to write anyway. The letters are addressed to different people from different walks of life, to his family members and to three generations of writers, from Ezra Pound to Robert Lowell to Lawrence Ferlinghetti.

In fact, I cannot think of any better way to end my tribute to this great old man than by quoting a few excerpts from his letters written to me over the years, which bring out the depth of his personality much better than any words of mine.

> I sent the Autobiography today or, rather, I wrote today to my agent at Random House to mail it to you at once. You'll get it in about a month, I suppose. It hasn't sold very well, only about 4 to 5 thousand. Some people like it and some hate it, say it's sloppily written and uninteresting from a literary viewpoint. I'm amused at the different aspects of it that people comment on, everybody that likes it likes it for a different reason. Ezra Pound spoke of the detailed revelations of incidents in the lives of people he knew that it contained, etc. I hope you find it worthwhile or at least amusing. It's meant to be casual, a day to day account of some of the happenings of my existence. The inferences lie deeper if you care to look for them. The general conclusion is that I was an unhappy youth and that I have grown up to be a very disappointed man. What do you think? (Jan 29, 1952)[22]

> You speak of your mother. It makes me think of mine. Not that they can be like each other, they probably are not, or that they may have been like each other (since mine is dead), but my attitude towards my own mother must be very much like your attitude to yours.... My only feeling was an inexpressible admiration coupled with an anger at not doing more, which I could not afford without turning my life into a slavery.... she ruined herself for her sons – but she did it in such a way that I was furious at her.... well, she's gone now, at 92 years of age. My father died at an age 3 years younger than I am now. He seems a young man to me. (May 29, 1951)[23]

---

22 *Why Should I Write a Poem Now*, 86–87.

23 Ibid., 83.

And in one of his last letters written in 1958, he wrote:

> Nothing can bridge the gap of distance and years for us except the written word, letters and without some knowledge of the intimacies of your life in India, even that becomes more and more difficult. I saw and heard the Indian musicians in Jim Laughlin's apartment last year, but without you to interpret for me, I could not be certain of their significance.... And as for modern music, the modern music I heard at the Brandeis spring festival last year, it was really abhorrent to me. Rock and Roll retains its interest but that is only primitive, which the African natives do better. The Parisian school of saxophone and clarinet is the only live thing hereabouts. Come to Paris when we can at least talk over the telephone. You'll hear from me at once via the book of letters or the photo if the mails permit it.[24]

24 Ibid., 110.

PREFACE TO *SELECTED POEMS*

Though the poem 'Sometimes' was written in Berkeley, California, in 1948 and the poem 'An Ordinary Life' was written in Secunderabad, India, in 1995, the seventy-odd poems in this collection still touch me and make sense to me. Most of them have not been published before in book form, although some have appeared in *Bones and Distances* (1968) and *Married Love* (1972), both published by Writers Workshop in Calcutta.

As I say in one of my poems, life has been mostly a matter of living the days. Except perhaps for that special occasion, the splitting of the brain into the myriad moments of intensity and feeling that perhaps give rise to what is a poem. Not that there is a poem in every one of those outbursts. Sometimes a precious word with its special meaning sits on the page staring back at you, asking to be written down. These poems are not of that kind. Many of them have been conceived over days and written over and over again, but the actual birth of the poem has been like the first spark of semen that shoots out, uncontrollable, at the climactic moment.

Many years ago, when I was about seventeen or eighteen, my one ambition was to be a great poet, but I did not know what it meant except to thrill at a line of Auden or a word of Wallace Stevens, and imagine the unimaginable – that one day I, too, would join their galaxy. Poets were lonely people, I had heard, and was I not the loneliest of the lonely? Poets had their minds full of words and thoughts of unimagined beauty or ugliness. Was not my mind so often a garden full of flowers or a cesspool full of filth that I could not dare look into the mirror? Poets drank a lot... yes, I had qualified by every known standard. Except perhaps that I could not sit down to write a poem. There they were, in the mind, the beautiful unbelievables, the fire and the flame burning within me. But the minute I put pen to paper, a million trite words would rush out. And so it would remain, a solitary word or a single line to convey the magnificence of my unwritten poem. So I hope that these poems, read by someone removed from my person, my mind, and the time and context in which they were written, contain some of this mystique, and give satisfaction – no, not that, but rather pleasure, that only words can convey, with or without their meaning. Why do I write? Because I like to write, because the words which I use convey the meaning and the feeling that I wish to convey, and the reader wishes to understand. Primarily the need is mine. I need to write just like I need to eat or sleep or fornicate. As far as readers are concerned, a majority of one is OK with me.

I think I have achieved most of what I wanted to achieve. I reached the top of my profession (as a civil engineer in the Government); I published a magazine in English from a remote town in India during the fifties, EAST AND WEST, to which a leading English-language newspaper devoted its entire centre page under the title 'A Surprise from Secunderabad;' I published two books of English poetry in the days when Indian English was not acceptable to the Cambridge crowd. The magazine EAST AND WEST, which I started with Kenneth Pettitt, an American friend, and my own meagre finances, was a satisfying but frustrating experience. I foresaw its inevitable end but that did not detract from the beauty and trauma of its birth. I knew it would be so. People told me so. THE LITTLE REVIEW and TRANSITION and PENGUIN NEW WRITING[25]

---

25 *The Penguin New Writing*, founded by John Lehmann as a continuation of *New Wriring*, was a monthly literary magazine issued over ten years (1940–50) in paperback format. Seventeen issues are in the Rayaprol's book collection at the University of Hyderabad.

had also gone the same way. But while it was alive it was very much so. People called it a legend. It attracted the attention of Mulk Raj Anand and Khushwant Singh, who were the great gods of Indian English writing in those days, and of Henry Miller and William Carlos Williams from America, who contributed to it, and a host of younger writers who like myself were struggling to articulate.

Looking back on all this, I feel that life has always been eluding me. I and Chris[26] were the dream children, walking down Kingsway in Secunderabad, dreaming of the world. We lived in a second-class city in middle-class families but we had big ambitions. We felt we were the stuff genius is made of, and there was some truth in that. We had problems of money, and understanding parents, conventions, and moronic companions and many moments of dullness. But we were there first. The Beardsley Prints of Wilde's Salome, Auden's abracadabra with the words:

> High up in this vertiginous crows-nest above
> Will you let us know what goes on in the world below,[27]

Eliot's special magic, Dylan Thomas's burning fire, all this was with us and more. With what perverse pleasure did we read of Herr Issywoo's Berlin stories, when our companions were

---

26 See note 10, p. 123.

27 The exact quote is ' ... please remember us / So high up here in this vertiginous / Crow's-nest of the earth. Perhaps you'll let us know / If anything happens in the world below', and it is not by Auden but by Louis MacNeice. It appears in 'Letter to Graham and Anna', originally in Auden's and MacNeice's *Letters from Iceland* (1937), and reprinted on page 49 of MacNeice's *Collected Poems 1925-1948* (Oxford University Press, 1963), a copy of which is in the Rayaprol's book collection at the University of Hyderabad.

flaunting Somerset Maugham or James Hilton. For we were the outsiders, the brilliant people, not left out but standing away from the crowds, because we... KNEW.

But as the years have gone by and I am safely ensconced in the world of wood, I have realized, indeed rather painfully, that I am no longer the genius that I thought I was. And now that there is such a spate of Indian English writing, and handsome books of poetry are coming out every year, I no longer am part of the scene. I no longer wish to talk of the I. On the verge of 70, I do not have much more to live for. But I am proud to have lived in those years, seen the glorious era of Hollywood and proud to belong to the times of Eliot and Auden, Sartre and Schweitzer, Sophia Loren and Marlon Brando, Tennessee Williams and Dylan Thomas, Satyajit Ray and Madhubala.[28] And I am deeply grateful to many people whom I have known, who have helped me realize myself and find fulfilment of a sort. Raymond Burnier and Alain Daniélou of Benares, Gayelord Hauser of Hollywood, Gilbert Neiman, Max Lazarus and Ray Perkins of Denver, Colorado, Kenneth Pettitt and Barbara Jean Holmes from Berkeley, Ted Warren and Yvor Winters from Stanford, William Carlos Williams from Rutherford, N. J., James Laughlin from New York, Nair from Prague, C. R. Mandy, Khushwant Singh and A. S. Raman from the *Illustrated Weekly of India*, P. Lal and Buddhadeva Bose from Calcutta, Jagmohan from Delhi, Christopher Sripada from Secunderabad, not to mention countless friends and companions from Secunderabad, Benares, Ranchi, my father and mother, my brother Rajasekhar, my sister Lalitha and a host of relatives who have been part of my life.[29] And

---

28 Indian film actress Mumtaz Jehan Begum Dehlavi (1933-1969), popularly known as Madhubala or Madhu.

29 German-born nutritionist and self-help author Gayelord Hauser (1895–1984) moved to Hollywood in 1927, where he became popular

finally to my wife Rajeswari, who has borne with me these forty-odd years through thick and thin, and my three graces Anu, Manu and Apu with their spouses and children.

---

among movie people. Author and translator Gilbert Neiman (1912-77) was one of Rayaprol's best friends in the United States. Max Leon Lazarus (1892-1961) was a German-Jewish painter who relocated to the Unites States to escape Nazi persecution. He first settled in St. Louis, Missouri, and eventually moved to Denver, where he met Rayaprol in 1950-51. In a letter dated 25 June 1950 to William Carlos Williams, Rayaprol mentions a 'rather out of the ordinary disc jockey' named Ray Perkins, who 'plays two hours of popular and horrid music on one of the local stations', despite the fact that he is a talented pianist (*Why Should I Write a Poem Now*, 60-61). Both Kenneth Pettitt and Barbara Jean Holmes were graduates of the University of California Berkeley. A(vadhanam) S(ita) Raman (1919-) and Khushwant Sing (1915-2014) were the first two Indian editors of the *Illustrated Weekly of India*, succeeding the Irish-born C.R. Mandy. P(urishottama) Lal (1929-2010) was the founder and publisher of the Writers Workshop, which issued Rayaprol's three poetry books. Both he and Bengali poet and writer Buddhadeva Bose (1908-74) contributed to *East and West*. Jagmohan may be the Indian politician Jagmohan Malhotra (born 1927), who served as Lieutenant Governor of Delhi and Goa, governor of Jammu and Kashmir, and minister of Urban Planning, Urban Development and Poverty Alleviation, and Tourism and Culture.

NOTES

I. *Poems*

THE RAIN: Enclosed with a letter from Rayaprol to Williams, 25 March 1950. See *Why Should I Write a Poem Now: The Letters of Srinivas Rayaprol and William Carlos Williams, 1949–1958*, ed. G. Krätli (Albuquerque, NM: The University of New Mexico Press, 2018), 156.

UNTITLED: (fragment). Enclosed with a letter from Rayaprol to Williams, 16 May 1955. *Why Should I Write a Poem Now*, 94.

UNTITLED: From 'A Bit of Me', *The Miscellany* (Calcutta [Kolkata]), no. 49 (February 1972): 30.

FOUR LOVE POEMS: First published as 'Three Love Poems', *Poetry* 93, No. 4 (January 1959): 224–5, with a note stating that the poems were translated from the Telugu by the author. They are reprinted in *Bones and Distances*, without any references to them being a translation and as the second, third, and fourth of the 'Four Love Poems'.

ORANGES ON A TABLE: *East and West* 5 (Autumn 1959): 54.

A LETTER TO EZRA POUND: Enclosed with a letter from Rayaprol to Williams, 24 December 1950. *Why Should I Write a Poem Now*, 165–6.

LES SALTIMBANQUES: *East and West* 5 (Autumn 1959): 55.

UNDER THE BO-TREE: Enclosed with a letter from Rayaprol to Williams, 10 June 1950. *Why Should I Write a Poem Now*, 162–3. In *Selected Poems* it has no dedication and forms the second of the 'Two Poems for the Buddha.'

LEGEND: Enclosed (with no title) with a letter from Rayaprol to Williams, 25 March 1950. *Why Should I Write a Poem Now*,

157-58. *Poetry* 79, no. 4 (January 1952): 198–9 (with the title 'Legend').

THE MAN WHO DIED OF A FEVER: *Poetry* 79, no. 4 (January 1952): 198. Reprinted in *Perspective of India: An Atlantic Monthly Supplement* 192, no. 4 (October 1953): 149.

PASTORALE: This may be one of the two poems which Rayaprol enclosed with his first letter to Williams (dated 22 October 1949), and of which Williams (on 12 February 1950) says: 'These are good, unevenly good but good. I think they should be printed' (*Why Should I Write a Poem Now*, 155–6).

YELLOW AND BLUE: Enclosed with a letter from Rayaprol to Williams, 22 April 1950. *Why Should I Write a Poem Now*, 158–9. A shorter version titled, 'A Question of Old Rains', is the first of two 'Poems for Jamini Roy' published in *Accent* (Winter 1951): 41 (the other is 'The Blue Woman'). In *Bones and Distances* the first and third stanzas form the second of the two 'Poems for the Painter.' In *Selected Poems* it precedes 'The Blue Woman' as a separate poem.

THIS IS JUST TO SAY: *East and West* 5 (Autumn 1959): 57–8.

NAGARJUNAKONDA: *The Miscellany* (Calcutta [Kolkata]) 48 (December 1971): 72.

POEM: Enclosed with a letter from Rayaprol to Williams, 10 June 1950 (with the title 'Lines for a Mother'). *Why Should I Write a Poem Now*, 161-62. *East and West* 5 (Autumn 1959): 55–6.

SHAKUNTALA: Enclosed with a letter from Rayaprol to Williams, 24 December 1950. *Why Should I Write a Poem Now*, 163–5.

STREETS: *Indian Literature* 29, no. 4 (114) (July-August, 1986): 56.

OLD RAIN: Enclosed (as 'Old Rains') with a letter from Rayaprol to Williams, 24 December 1950. *Why Should I Write a Poem Now*, 164-65. *Quest* 1, no. 3 (December 1955 – January 1956): 22–3.

FOR JOHN EVERYMAN, POET: Enclosed with a letter from Rayaprol to Williams, 10 June 1950. *Why Should I Write a Poem Now*, 160–1.

TO AN EDITOR: 'A Bit of Me', *The Miscellany* (Calcutta [Kolkata]), no. 49 (February 1972): 31.

IT RAINS SOFTLY ON THE CITY: *East and West* 5 (Autumn 1959): 58–9 (with the title 'Incidences').

THE WIDOW IN WASHINGTON SQUARE: This is the title in *Bones and Distances*. In *Selected Poems* it is simply 'The Widow.'

2. *Translations*

THE TRAIN YOU WOULD WISH TO TAKE (Arudra): *East and West* 1, no. 1 (Spring 1956): 34–5; *Modern Telugu Poetry*, ed. A. Chaya Devi (Hyderabad: Kavita, 1956), 30.

A POEM (Sri Sri): *East and West* 1, no. 1 (Spring 1956): 35–6; *Modern Indian Poetry: An Anthology*, ed. A.V. Rajeswara Rau (New Delhi: Kavita, 1958): 128.

SAD VOICES (Sri Sri): *East and West* 1, no. 5 (Autumn 1959): 46–7.

CALL ME BY A NAME (Sishtla): *East and West* 1, no. 1 (Spring 1956): 36–7; *Modern Telugu Poetry*, 17–19.

NOBODY NOWHERE (Ajanta): *East and West* 1, no. 1 (Spring 1956): 38-39; *Modern Telugu Poetry*, 26–7.

FROM VISHNUPARIJATAMU (Tarigonda Venkamamba): *Women Writing in India: 600 B.C. to the Present. Vol. I: 600 B.C. to the Early Twentieth Century*, ed. Susie Tharu and K. Lalita (New York: The Feminist Press, 1991 and 1993), 125–6.

JAILHOUSE CLOCK (Tallapragada Viswasundaramma).: *Women Writing in India*, Vol. I, 401.

MY STRICKEN VOICE (Nidumanuri Revati Devi): *Women Writing in India: 600 B.C. to the Present. Vol. II: The Twentieth Century*, ed. Susie Tharu and K. Lalita. 2 vols. (New York: The Feminist Press, 1991 and 1993), 580–1.

EMBERS OF HOPE (Nidumanuri Revati Devi): Ibid.

3. Prose

CITY OF MINE: Unpublished.

LOUIS MACNEICE: A MEETING BY THE RIVER: Unpublished.

TO STANFORD: Unpublished.

THE PHYSICS OF COLOUR: *Panchshila* (Bombay), January 1957, n.p. *East and West* 1, no. 4 (Summer 1957): 82–8.

HEART CONDITION: *Indian Literature* 27, no. 2 (March-April 1984): 108–12.

REMEMBERING WILLIAM CARLOS WILLIAMS: *The Journal of Indian Writing in English* (Gulbarga [Kalaburagi], Karnataka) 22, no. 2 (1994): 1–10.

PREFACE: S. Rayaprol, *Selected Poems* (Calcutta: Writers Workshop, 1995): 9–12.

AFTERWORD

Modernism is essentially a question of language, in Wittgenstein's famed postulate, shaping and signifying the limits of our world. That is, language as a matter of limits, endlessly on the edge – as well as on the verge – of meaning, representational or otherwise – boundary-bound. To appreciate the 'modern difference', with all its artistic prospects and implications, its infinite fault lines, fissures and ruptures, we should consider the extent to which modernity expanded, altered or even dissolved the limits of our known world, and the many ways in which modernism – in all its forms, versions and variants – actualized and interpreted such a transformation, translating the new world into new language(s). In so doing, it blurred or erased traditional bounds and limits – linguistic and stylistic as well as cultural and geographic – recasting the artist into a constant expatriate or no-land's man, free to choose his own models and masters, and to pursue creation as a perpetual and peripatetic act of departure. 'We who leave the house in April, Lord, / How shall we return?'[30] Nissim Ezekiel's question contains its own inevitable answer in the time of departure, April being the month when 'folk long to go on pilgrimage' as well as the 'cruelest month' of Eliot's departure from the house of Edwardian and Georgian poetry. In this comfortable and familiar (if stifling) abode:

30 Nissim Ezekiel, 'A Time to Change', in *Collected Poems, 1952–1988* (Oxford: Oxford University Press, 1989), 4.

the scene was set; it repeated what
Was in the script.
Then the theatre was changed
To something else. Its past was a souvenir.[31]

The theatre was changed because the act of leaving one's house coincides always, inevitably, with the annihilation of the house itself (as a compound of multiple and overlapping identities, national, linguistic, cultural, etc.) and its decisive and definitive replacement with the stage as a place of constant change and infinite role-playing. It was changed, too, because the stage always changes to accommodate a new play, to entertain a new audience, to keep the illusion alive. Like Stevens' 'poem of the mind', the modern poet as expatriate and permanent nonresident has 'to learn the speech of the place' and 'find what will suffice' in order to 'construct a new stage' and 'be on that stage'[32].

Building a new stage and being on it – or, in Pound's words, 'testing the language and its adaptability to certain modes'[33] – adds a definite experiential and experimental dimension to the character of the poet (and the poem), which is consistent with the expatriate condition and its predicaments. However, anglophone Indian poets never really or fully inhabited the same house that was abandoned by Eliot, Pound, Stevens, Williams and their modernist contemporaries and disciples. What they knew, instead, was a colonial surrogate, a literary equivalent of Victorian and Edwardian architecture overseas, in which they lived as occupants or guests until postmodernity

31 Wallace Stevens, 'Of Modern Poetry', in *The Collected Poems of Wallace Stevens* (New York: Alfred A. Knopf, 1954), 239-40.

32 Ibid.

33 Ezra Pound, 'A Retrospect', in *Pavannes and Divisions* (New York: Alfred A. Knopf, 1918), 107.

and postcolonialism finally changed the rules of occupancy. But even as official residents, anglophone Indian poets continued – and continue – to live culturally and linguistically *ex patria*, their 'new stage' consisting of materials adopted and adapted from different traditions, autochthonous as well as imported.

Of course, an artist's freedom to choose his own models depends upon the availability of alternative models to choose from. For the modern Indian poet, this opportunity came first with travel and residence abroad, and later also with the growing availability in India of Western literature, Hollywood movies and American popular music. Whether encountered abroad or experienced at home, these alternative models and cultural imports combined with older poetic traditions in the regional languages to bring about a new poetic sensibility, which used modernism as a flexible paradigm and a blueprint for cross-pollination, assimilation and development. Modernism, in fact, tends to be flexible, catholic and open-ended enough to accommodate all kinds of poetic traditions, modes and influences, including periodical returns to form and meter. All these movements forward, backward and sideward, all these fault lines, fissures and ruptures are not only present in modern anglophone Indian poetry as a whole, but they can also be found in the work of a single poet, if not in the same collection or even the same poem.

The peculiar position of Srinivas Rayaprol is a case in point. As one of a handful of anglophone poets who, in the first couple of decades after the Independence, imparted a new course to Indian poetry by negotiating and assimilating (or rejecting) the influences of European and Anglo-American Modernism, he must have felt the weight of this conspicuous elephant in the room.

Rayaprol was born R.S. Marthandam on October 25, 1925, in Secunderabad (Hyderabad), Andhra Pradesh (now Telangana), the son of prominent Telugu poet and academic

Rayaprolu Subbarao (1892-1984). He studied at Nizam College in Hyderabad, Banaras Hindu University in Varanasi, and Stanford University in California, earning a master's degree in Civil Engineering in 1950. While at Stanford, his poetic leanings prompted him to attend a creative course taught by the influential critic Yvor Winters. When Winters, a repentant modernist turned formalist, proved unsupportive of his poetic efforts but also introduced him to the poetry of William Carlos Williams, Rayaprol decided to write to the renowned poet-pediatrician in Rutherford, New Jersey, thus initiating a decade-long epistolary relationship which provides an Indian variant to the Pater-Son model Williams pursued with younger (male) poets, most notably Allen Ginsberg[34]. In the spring of 1951, after working for almost a year at the U.S. Bureau of Reclamation in Denver, Colorado, Rayaprol returned to India to pursue a career as civil engineer in the public sector. There he married, had three daughters, and settled in what he would call 'the world of wood', a professionally and socially respectable existence, although one spoiled by cultural isolation, intellectual restlessness, and the burden of 'terrible ambitions' unfulfilled. Stuck in 'a town where everything happens elsewhere', or working for months at a time in remote locations, he shared 'with Kafka … the loneliness of the writer who has to pursue another occupation through the better part of his life'. Yet, in spite of the circumstances, he managed to publish three collections of poetry and a short-lived yet important literary magazine, *East and West* (1956-59), to contribute poems to various publications in India and abroad, and to maintain a prolonged correspondence with poets and writers, editors and publishers in the United

34 See *Why Should I Write a Poem Now: The Letters of Srinivas Rayaprol and William Carlos Williams, 1949-1958*, ed. Graziano Krätli (Albuquerque, NM: The University of New Mexico Press, 2018).

States: Williams first and foremost, but also James Laughlin (Williams' publisher), Karl Shapiro (*Poetry*'s editor in the early 1950s), and Gilbert Neiman (who helped Rayaprol publish his first poems in American magazines, including *Poetry*). Yet his literary career and poetic achievement ultimately reflect a deep sense of isolation, of being bogged down by provincial mediocrity, and cut off from what Rayaprol saw as his chosen cultural homeland – not Bombay, Calcutta, Delhi, or Madras, but New York and, especially, Paris.

In what would be his last book, *Selected Poems*, published three years before his untimely death on December 7, 1998, Rayaprol inserted a pair of footnotes supposedly meant to clarify, if not justify or explain, the peculiar treatment of one theme, love, and the conspicuous absence of another, 'Indianness', in his work. Whether we take Rayaprol's arguments at face value or not, these two themes represent the twin pillars standing at the gateway of his poetry, signifying its content while suggesting a possible key to its understanding (or, depending on the approach, misunderstanding). Ultimately, it is up to the reader (and to each individual reader by and for himself or herself only) to find out if such a key will actually unlock any doors, and if these doors will reveal meaningful rooms, or further conceal what lies behind them.

Selected Poems consists of forty-two 'Later Poems' (some actually written as early as 1950), followed by Rayaprol's previous two collections, *Bones and Distances* (1968) and *Married Love and Other Poems* (1972). The two footnotes appear halfway through the first section of the book and serve as a lead-in to the poems that follow.

The first note is appended to a poem whose title sounds vaguely like a personal manifesto but de facto reveals a self-exploratory – and self-diagnostic – attitude that is frequent in Rayaprol's poetry. Coming after a dreary, six-poem sequence about death and dying, 'I Am All That I Love' lists (in reverse chronological order) the four individuals who are, we must assume, the prime receivers of the poet's love, namely Rayaprol's mentor William Carlos Williams (the 'doctor'), his best friend Christoph (i.e., Murthi V.N. Sripada), his father (the 'absent one'), and his 'dear mother', whom the poet 'almost forgot' to mention, but simply because love 'is such a funny thing [that] when you / Feel it most you least can tell'. Father, father figure, and mother are then mentioned (in this order) in the footnote, which further expounds and complicates the poet's idea of love:

> I have this thing about love. A kind of *idée fixe*. That it has nothing to do with sex, that its expression is always inadequate and falls short of the feeling itself, that it is sad and tender and beautiful, full of sacrifices and completely undemanding.
>
> And yet how to divest it from this other feeling, this possessiveness, this hunger, this physical torment of absence, this wanting between the thighs.
>
> This has been the problem always.
>
> And so I have loved, with equal intensity and passion, and at different times, my father, 66-year-old Doc Williams, my wife, the Adivasi child on the streets of Ranchi, Picasso's naked ugliness, Kruschev's [*sic*] face in *Time* and Tennessee William's [*sic*] women.[35]

The note is self-explanatory yet elusive. The first paragraph introduces an idealized concept of love that finds expression in various literary forms and traditions (including Rayaprol's

35 S. Rayaprol, *Selected Poems* (Calcutta: Writers Workshop, 1995), 31.

father's version of Platonic love, *amalina śṛṅgāra*, which inspired a Romantic turn in Telugu poetry); the second acknowledges the limits and fallacy of such a concept, and sees real life as a constant and brutal battle between the spirit and the flesh; and the third provides a short, emblematic list of people whom Rayaprol has loved 'with equal intensity and passion, and at different times'. In addition to the already mentioned triad, this list includes 'the Adivasi child on the streets of Ranchi, Picasso's naked ugliness, Khrushchev's face in *Time* and Tennessee William's [*sic*] women'. The inclusion of the Adivasi child, Picasso's naked ugliness, Khrushchev's face, and Tennessee Williams' female characters expands and complicates Rayaprol's idea of love, forgoing the dualism of flesh and spirit to suggest a far more intricate and provocative form of esthetic appreciation, which is elaborated (with mixed results) in the three poems that come immediately after the footnote. All three proclaim the poet's physical attraction to the male body as portrayed in magazine photographs. However, there is a significant cultural difference between the first two poems, 'All Kinds of Love' and 'For Mulk Raj Anand', which address Old World iconic figures shown at some stage of physical decline ('Fat old men with flat white faces'), and the third, 'All American', which praises sarcastically the superficial virtues of a New World type, 'The kind of face / that photographs so well in *Time*', especially in advertisements and glamour shots. Far more complex and problematic is the message that the first two poems seem to convey, in comparison with the relatively straightforward statement of the third. In the suggestively titled 'All Kinds of Love', the poet's stated attraction to fat, old male bodies that 'shine out of the pages of *Time*', leads to some rather convoluted meditation on the need to descend in the crucible of carnal knowledge in order to achieve a state of intellectual communion or spiritual kinship. In 'For Mulk Raj Anand', however, the process seems to be inverted, and the 'wholly physical' fascination that Anand's 'ravaged face / and luminous eyes' hold for the poet 'is just another way / to say / that our minds have met / a long while ago'. In Rayaprol's idiosyncratic *saison en enfer*, the torment of the flesh to attain 'peace with the flesh' is an endless trial as well as its memory. To further complicate the ambiguous relationship between physical attraction and esthetic appreciation, in 'For Mulk Raj Anand' Rayaprol makes it clear that the similarities between Picasso and the Indian novelist extend to their art, and the ugliness of their bare bodies is but an indication of their respective achievement in exposing 'beauty in ugliness'. Consequently, we may read the four lines 'Your ravaged face / and luminous eyes / burn into me / from the page' in both a literal and a metaphorical way, depending on the meaning we attribute to the word 'page'. In the former case, it is the page of the magazine showing the photograph of the novelist; in the latter, it is the page of one of the groundbreaking novels – *Untouchable* (1935) and *Coolie* (1936) in particular – in which Anand showed beauty (the 'luminous eyes') in the ugliness of degrading social conditions (the 'ravaged face').

Besides 'For Mulk Raj Anand', five other poems in this section have titles that suggest Indian subjects: 'Sunrise over Kamareddy', 'Nagarjunkonda', 'Godhuli Time', 'Diwali Days' and 'Shakuntala'. This, however, is just a pretext, or an appearance, as Rayaprol claims in the second footnote, which is about a different kind of love, no less problematic and difficult to define, but with a broader cultural relevance.

Candid statements or concerns about 'Indianness' frequently tinged the political and intellectual debates of the newly independent nation. When they involved poetry, fiction, and other forms of creative writing, their outcome was usually affected by an excessive and overzealous emphasis on the linguistic rather than the literary medium. More often than not, the use of English (still largely seen as a foreign idiom) versus a native language, like the choice of non-nativist subjects, overshadowed more sensible critical approaches to a writer's work.

Rayaprol's footnote about Indianness consists of two related statements that, because of their implications, need to be addressed separately. The first is straightforward enough and makes a point that may be applied to landscape poetry in general, regardless of cultural or historical circumstances:

> I have been asked about the Indianness of my poems. And I am puzzled and do not know what to say. I have never thought that a poem required 'racial' characteristics. I have written a poem titled 'Sunrise over Kamareddy' but the poem was about the Landscape of the Heart.[36]

Rayaprol may have used 'racial' ironically, if not provocatively, since he put it in quotation marks and provided an example that involves nothing more 'racial' than a location in his native state. More likely, though, he meant to subsume and signify the whole range of vernacular themes recurrent in Indian poetry, anglophone and otherwise, before and after the Independence, for which 'cultural and geographical characteristics' might have been a more appropriate definition. As a matter of fact, most postcolonial anglophone poets wrote at least a few (and some more than a few) poems with archeological, historical, mythological, literary, artistic, or other 'culturally specific' subjects and themes. Rayaprol himself enclosed at least five 'Indian' poems to letters he sent to Williams in March, April, June, and December 1950.[37]

Subject and theme, however, are only partially representative of a poem's cultural and geographical characteristics. Where a

---

36 Ibid., 39.

37 See *Why Should I Write a Poem Now*, 155ff.

poet writes *from* is always more important and meaningful than what he or she writes (or claims to write) *about*, which may be occasional, delusive, or imaginary. There is, for instance, an Indianness of the English language, which combines cultural appropriation, artistic license, and sometimes inadequate editing (not to mention the fact that multilingual poets may write in English but think in another language, mentally translating back and forth, or in and out) – all behaviors of which Rayaprol's poetry provides eloquent and occasionally problematic examples.

However, the heart may be an undiscovered country, but is never really nobody's land:

> And yet, I suppose I cannot forget my birth, and somewhere lying deep below was a private hurt about this. What did I share with these people of my land? Not the language or their ways or their thoughts. Certainly not the time-old habits, which if they had some sense in those days, were now nothing but examples of their cruelty, their lack of consideration for others, their utter disregard for kindness.[38]

Written more than four decades after his return to India, this second statement reflects Rayaprol's bitter disillusion and estrangement with his own country and life there. Yet, these are more or less the same feelings that he conveyed to his American correspondents as early as 1951, that is, only a few months after his repatriation. Much of this negativity had to do with the simple trauma of being back, the difficulties of adjusting to a life that he had largely outlived (or so he felt at the time), and the consequent sense of displacement and despair. 'What the hell did you expect?' replied Williams on 29 January 1952 to a letter (now lost) in which Rayaprol must

38 *Selected Poems*, 39.

have vented his frustrations. 'Did you think that India was going to be a picnic for you?'[39]

Soon, however, as he starts working as a civil engineer, new frustrations and new doubts arise. On July 6, 1951, he writes from Ranchi, Bihar (now Jharkhand):

> I have left the cruel comfort of my home to take a job at a place a thousand miles away and quite God-forsaken as far as I am concerned … I never felt such a foreigner, never this sense of being excluded and discriminated against as here.[40]

The letter is addressed to a friend whom, only a few months before, he had urged to 'come to Paris. There is no city like it in the whole world that I have seen. Certainly no city that I can wish for you as this one'.[41] Now the harsh reality of Nehruvian India – on the one hand, traditional life, looking backward but representing the backbone of the country; on the other, looking forward, economic planning, large infrastructural projects, the Green Revolution – started to hit him hard. '[H]ere in this remote village where cleanliness is unheard of and people live as a matter of habit, here I feel lost and confused and wonder: Is this my country? What do I share with them?'[42] It is the same question Rayaprol will repeat four decades later in the footnote on the Indianness of his poems. The answer he gives in 1995 ('Not the language, etc.') is drastic, uncompromising and opens a deep cleft that is ultimately the space out of which his poetry is written.

---

39 *Why Should I Write a Poem Now*, 86.

40 Rayaprol to Gilbert Neiman, 6 July 1951. Unpublished. The letters between Rayaprol and Neiman are in the Gilbert Neiman Papers, Clarion University.

41 Rayaprol to Gilbert Neiman, 6 March 1951. Unpublished.

42 Rayaprol to Gilbert Neiman, 6 July 1951. Unpublished.

This space, in which he has been digging himself deeper and deeper over the years, dates back to his time in America, where he felt he was 'always a foreigner enjoying both the benefits and the disfavor which go with being one', as he wrote to Williams from Denver in the spring of 1950.[43] The space that would become his own, poetically as well as existentially, was already taking shape. He didn't recognize it, or not as such, until years later, when he found himself a stranger in his own country and was finally able to name it. He had become (the example of 'lonely, lonely Ezra Pound' providing the impulse and the inspiration) 'Always the foreigner now'.

There is a telling difference between Rayaprol's earlier and later Indian poems. While the few from his time in America show a genuine if vague attempt to engage with themes that are traditional ('Legend'), religious ('Under the Bo-Tree', 'Buddha'), literary or artistic ('Shakuntala', 'Poems for the Painter'), those he penned in spare time while 'building dams, powerhouses and the like' tend to be autobiographical, reflective, nostalgic, despondent, even (a bit narcissistically) resentful of being a literary has-been. They are also more incisive, explicit, and indicative of the space he is writing from, the double foreign-ness he has embraced as his own true identity and poetic voice.

The poem that most emblematically represents this space is perhaps 'Godhuli Time', in which Rayaprol uses a favorite Indian subject to distance himself, culturally as well as emotionally, from Indian village life, its idyllic depiction, and the 'national poetry' it inspired in the period before and after the Independence. Instead of the poetic dust raised by the cows returning from the fields, Rayaprol notes the discomfort caused by dense smoke and the smell of burned milk. In the second stanza, the voyeuristic experience of surprising two

---

43 *Why Should I Write a Poem Now*, 42.

young lovers increases his stranger-ness. And in the third and final, darkness follows a train seen in the distance: a most intrusive presence in a pastoral landscape, and the opposite of the ox-cart with which Sarojini Naidu – one of India's true national poets – concludes her own *godhuli vela* poem, 'June Sunset', published three decades before the Independence. In Rayaprol's poem, the lighted windows of the fleeting train suggest the heightened intimacy provided by a home away from home, and find a counterpart in the flickering lights that beckon man and bird and beast home. And while the train reminds the visitor of his coming to the village, his thoughts travel in the opposite direction, towards the home that he never had. Nothing could be more removed from Naidu's Victorian-Orientalist imagery:

> Here shall my heart find its haven of calm,
> By rush-fringed rivers and rain-fed streams
> That glimmer thro' meadows of lily and palm.
> Here shall my soul find its true repose
> Under a sunset sky of dreams
> Diaphanous, amber and rose.[44]

Instead of flickering lights and the lighted windows of a fleeting train, 'June Sunset' ends 'poetically', with a glimmer of 'faint stars gleam[ing] in the eastern sky / To herald a rising moon'.

Rayaprol's choice of the same, cherished locale and time of day marks a dramatic point of departure from Naidu's glowing tableau. The home that he never had is the house of language and literary tradition, the one which a poet like Naidu still inhabited – or at least evoked – with a reasonable degree of confidence, but of which Rayaprol's contemporary Nissim

---

44 S. Naidu, 'June Sunset', in *The Broken Wing: Songs of Love, Death and Destiny, 1915-1916* (London: Heinemann, 1919), 66–67.

Ezekiel, writing just a few years before him, asked: 'We who leave the house in April, Lord / How shall we return?' To Rayaprol, the answer to such a question was clear, and clearly, even ingeniously articulated in a poem like 'Godhuli Time'.

The radical difference between Rayaprol's and Naidu's rendering of the same subject may be attributed, naturally, to a generation gap, although most of Naidu's subjects celebrating Indian rural life and folklore continued to shape anglophone Indian poetry (and poetics) long after the Independence, filling an excessive number of 'Indo-Anglian' or 'Indian English' anthologies with bucolic bliss, traditions and customs. Exactly the 'time-old habits' which Rayaprol condemns as being antiquated 'examples of cruelty, lack of consideration for others [and] utter disregard for kindness'. Yet we should remember that, at the time of Rayaprol's writing, Indian village life was still largely seen as a preferred if not recommended subject for artists and writers, and one cannot deny that it has inspired a number of remarkable works of art and literature.

When the Oxford-educated, London-based, 21-one-year-old Dom Moraes met Nehru in Delhi at the end of 1959, and told him about his plan to write a book about India, the Pandit's reaction was clear and to the point: 'You must go to the villages and live with the villagers. You must accept them for what they are. They are good people'[45]. Needless to say, Moraes the poet kept safely away from the villages, and even when he covered rural India as a journalist, the experience does not seem to have affected his poetry in any remarkable way. Perhaps his professional outlook helped him keep poetry and prose apart, and he dealt with subjective and objective realities using different literary languages and media, while Rayaprol struggled to reconcile his daytime profession and

---

45 Dom Moraes, *Gone Away: An Indian Journal* (London: Heinemann, 1960), 64.

his nighttime passion – or, as he put it in a letter to Karl Shapiro, the unbearable foreign-ness of being 'an engineer by profession and a poet by passion. Another of those sad cases'[46].

Always the foreigner now. What makes this state a severe and irreversible condition is not so much the noun as the three functional words that surround it and circumstantiate its meaning. In ascending order, they are: the definite article, indicating an absolute, ontological condition (not just *a foreigner* but *the foreigner*, like Camus' hero is not simply 'a stranger' but 'The Stranger'); the first adverb, *always*, which suggests perpetuity as well as continuity and invariability; and the second adverb, *now*, whose meaning is more ambiguous but also potentially more important since it implies a break between what came before (until *now*) from what may come after (from *now* on). So, we may ask, what caused the break between before and after, engineering Rayaprol's rebirth as a foreigner forever? The obvious answer is the three years he spent in America – 'the place of my birth (3 years ago)', as he wrote to Gilbert Neiman from New York City, on the eve of his departure[47] –, an intense, liberating experience that consolidated young R.S. Marthandam's poetic impulse and prompted him to adopt the pen name of Srinivas Rayaprol and pursue poetry against all odds. But America alone cannot account for the most obscure and problematic references in his poetry. Or, if it does, it is at a far deeper, far more personal and private level than what is commonly referred to as 'culture shock'.

By the time he managed to put his passion in print, and to produce a first volume of verse in 1968, the landscape of contemporary anglophone poetry in India had changed significantly enough to include, alongside Sarojini Naidu's children and grandchildren, a group of young, urban poets

46 *Why Should I Write a Poem Now*, 150.

47 Rayaprol to Gilbert Neiman, 20/21 February 1951. Unpublished.

whose idea of Indianness neither coincided with the ideal of the rural village and its 'time-old habits', nor was inspired by the nationalistic afflatus that had sustained their parents' and grandparents' struggle for independence. On the contrary, such an idea was shaped, on the one hand, by the many idiosyncrasies, challenges, and contradictions of the newly independent country on its arduous path toward modernization, and, on the other, by the modernist ideas these young poets had absorbed abroad, in Europe or the United States.

In 1968, besides *Bones and Distances*, Writers Workshop published Gauri Deshpande's *Between Births*, Kersey Katrak's *A Journal of the Way*, Pritish Nandy's *On Either Side of Arrogance*, and G.S. Sharat Chandra's *Bharata Natyam Dancer and Other Poems*, among others. By then, Nissim Ezekiel, Dom Moraes, Adil Jussawalla, Kamala Das, Gieve Patel, and A.K. Ramanujan had published their first – and, in some cases, major – collections (Ezekiel and Moraes starting as early as 1952 and 1953, respectively), while Arvind Krishna Mehrotra was experimenting with concrete poetry and little magazines, and Arun Kolatkar was publishing his first poems in English and Marathi, testing the expressive possibilities of translating them back and forth.

None of these poets 'went to the villages and lived with the villagers', and only a few actually paid more than a fleeting attention to rural India, and the results tend to be far less sympathetic and lyrical than anything written before, either in verse or in prose[48]. For the most part, they are urban, cosmopolitan and cutting-edge; their engagement is in a literary rather than a political cause, and their poetry explores

---

48 The most notable and iconoclastic example is, of course, *Jejuri*, Arun Kolatkar's account of a 'pilgrimage' to the temple town of Jejuri, in western Maharashtra. The book was first published in the magazine *Opinion Literary Quarterly* in 1974 and as a stand-alone volume two years later.

the psychodynamics and the psychogeographies of India's largest cities, especially Bombay and Calcutta.[49] However, while some of their poems expose the many problems and shortcomings of post-independence India, none of them seems to express their author's cynical disillusion in such explicit and blunt terms as Rayaprol's '10 Downing Street':

> Is this the India that I have come back to?
> – tempted by Gandhi's gospel and Nehru's call
> after centuries of slavery. Have we come to this?
> Bound by the shackles that we overthrew not so long ago.

So much for the sociopolitical side of things. As for the literary, on the facing page of *Selected Poems* is 'The Golden Gate', ending with a recommendation to 'all Indo-Anglians that are trying to vend / Their latest versions of our Great Culture / For the Western Vultures' (a scathing statement, although one that, to some extent, anticipates the success of anglophone Indian fiction in the global mass market). If this sounds too harsh, we should take into consideration the resentment that was nagging Rayaprol in the late 1980s, knowing that, unlike Vikram Seth, he had 'stayed behind in his native state' and tried to produce, if not a 'similar tome / Of similar happenings', certainly poetry worth this name (not to mention the international success that such a 'tome' had brought this 'fellow Stanfordian'). As Dom Moraes pointed out a few years later, reviewing Rayaprol's *Selected Poems*, 'Indian poetry in English has always been produced in the large cities: Bombay, Delhi, Calcutta, Madras. Had Rayaprol lived in one of these, it is possible that he would have found encouragement and incentive to continue as he began. That he failed to do so is

---

49 With the significant difference that Calcutta's literary modernism happened largely in Bengali.

attributable to the circumstances in which he lived'.

It is indeed possible that, had Rayaprol lived in Bombay, Calcutta, Delhi or Madras, he 'would have found encouragement and incentive to continue as he began'. However, the 'circumstances in which he lived' can only partially explain the elusive literary career of a poet whose work appears to be marked, since very early, by a peculiar sort of melancholic indulgence, a deep-seated sense of disappointment, narcissistic discontent, and the recurring idea of failure as a form of achievement, or vice versa.

In Rayaprol, what seems to have been 'the problem always' is not the insoluble conflict between *eros* and *philia* (or *eros* and *agape*), but the ongoing struggle to articulate 'the voice before and the voice after' without exposing the voice itself, its nature and – most important – its true source. Why so? Because this is the voice that must remain unnamed in order to name, and must be nurtured in order to germinate. It is the voice that exists – and can exist only – between suppression and expression, or speechlessness and speech. This is Rayaprol's veritable 'Landscape of the Heart', the voiceless space defined by what can only be voiced otherwise, by means of select key words (desire, deceit, betrayal, sinful, knot), metaphorical expressions, private allegories, and enigmatic images that often suggest a secret language, discreet and disturbing like the 'dormant hand that stirs the privacy of pain'.

To be effective in conveying *by way of* concealing, and vice versa, such a language has to be metaphoric as well as mimetic, and Rayaprol found suitable and affordable models in such favorite modernists as Williams, Stevens, and Pound, whose first canto ('Came we then to the bounds of deepest water') provided the pattern for the peculiar incipit of 'A Taste for Death' ('Shared we such a room / on Sherman Street'). On the strength and the authority of their example, he developed his own idiosyncratic versification, with uneven results: some quite original (and unlike anything else in contemporary anglophone Indian poetry); some rather eccentric; and some questionable or problematic, certainly difficult to justify as poetic license. Which raises the question whether Telugu, Rayaprol's mother tongue (and Rayaprol's father's literary medium), played a significant role in the mental process of poetic articulation. It is a hypothesis that, although virtually impossible to verify, could throw some light on Rayaprol's knotty and occasionally obscure poetic diction. However, when translating from the Telugu of other poets (older, contemporary, or younger), and dealing with someone else's demons rather than confronting his own, Rayaprol's diction appears to be freer of the sharp-edged and convoluted character that distinguishes most of his poetry. This typically allows for a more relaxed approach, which manifests itself in the adoption of lowbrow rather than high-modernist models, especially in the use of expressions culled from American movies and popular music ('you can't take it with you', 'lover come back to me', 'hush a bye my baby'). It is an original and provocative approach, and one that, only a few years later, will find more conscious and relevant expression in Kolatkar's Anglo-Marathi pulp diction ('listen baby / i get paid when i say so') and, through his example, Arvind Krishna Mehrotra's versions of Kabir's bhajans ('O pundit, your hairsplitting's / So much bullshit', 'That's the end of the story', 'It's a lot of crap')[50]. Culturally speaking, the source remains pretty much the same, but the sensibility changes with the times. What for Rayaprol was the landscaped front yard of Hollywood's golden years, for Kolatkar and Mehrotra, both sons of the Sixties, is the backyard and junkyard of hard-boiled fiction, rock music, and comic books.

---

50 *Songs of Kabir*, translated by Arvind Krishna Mehrotra (New York: New York Review of Books, 2011).

INDEX OF POEM TITLES

ACKNOWLEDGEMENTS

We would like to thank the Srinivas Rayaprol Literary Trust for their continual support, Arvind Krishna Mehrotra for his creative advice and matchmaking, and – last but not least – Michael Schmidt and Andrew Latimer of Carcanet Press for transmuting both support and advice into a concrete reality.